ENDORSEMENTS

"This Bible study series offers an excellent opportunity for spiritually mature women to come alongside younger or new Christian women who are willing to be taught and counseled. Together, they discover God's purpose and plan for their lives."
—**Susan Titus Osborn,** director, Christian Communicator Manuscript Critique Service and author of 29 books, including *Wounded by Words*

"You will benefit whether studying on your own or in a small group because of the wide-ranging elements. It has personal stories, thought-provoking questions, intriguing ideas for mentoring, and practical challenges to grow closer to God. Janet Thompson's heart for encouraging women comes through loud and clear."
—**Kathy Collard Miller,** speaker and author of *Women of the Bible* ("The Smart Guide to the Bible" Series)

"Janet Thompson has given us a clear road map to practical, biblically based mentoring in this series. God's scriptural ideals for mentoring are laid out clearly and concisely, with wisdom, wit, and vulnerability."
—**Kathi Macias,** author of *Mothers of the Bible Speak to Mothers of Today, Beyond Me,* and *How Can I Run a Tight Ship When I'm Surrounded by Loose Cannons?*

To my Beautiful Daughter,
Wendy Lea

All my love always —
Mom (!)

FACE-TO-FACE
BIBLE STUDY SERIES

FACE-TO-FACE WITH

MARY AND MARTHA

SISTERS in CHRIST

*Five Sessions for
Individuals, M&M'S (Mentors & Mentees, Friends, Family)
or Groups*

with

*Leader's Guide for Group-Study Facilitators,
with Session Guide*

JANET THOMPSON

NEW HOPE
PUBLISHERS
Birmingham Alabama

Mary and Martha: Sisters in Christ
By Janet Thompson

New Hope Publishers logo
Birmingham, Alabama

New Hope® Publishers
P. O. Box 12065
Birmingham, AL 35202-2065
www.newhopepublishers.com

New Hope Publishers is a division of WMU®.

Library of Congress Cataloging-in-Publication Data

Thompson, Janet, 1947-
    Face to face with Mary and Martha : sisters in Christ : five sessions for
individuals, M&M'S (mentors & mentees, friends, family) or groups ; with leader's
guide for group study facilitators and session guide / Janet Thompson.

        p. cm. -- (Face to face Bible study series)
    Includes bibliographical references and index.
    ISBN 978-1-59669-254-1 (sc : alk. paper)
    1. Mary, of Bethany, Saint. 2. Martha, Saint. 3. Christian women--Religious life--
Textbooks. 4. Mentoring--Religious aspects--Christianity--Textbooks. I. Title.

    BX8656.T53 2009
    226'.0071--dc22

                    2009003258

ISBN-10: 1-59669-254-5
ISBN-13: 978-1-59669-254-1
N094152 • 0609 • 4M1

DEDICATED WITH LOVE

To

Sisters in Christ,
breast cancer sisters,
and my *real* sister

TABLE OF CONTENTS

WELCOME

My Story

I began taking steps to start the Woman to Woman Mentoring Ministry while at my home church, Saddleback Church, in Lake Forest, California, pastored by Rick Warren. "Feed My sheep" was God's call and challenge to me to go into full-time ministry. God quickly revealed that *feeding* was mentoring and *the sheep* were women in churches all over the world. In obedience to the call, I launched the ministry in my home in January 1996, and we quickly outgrew my living room. After receiving numerous requests from other churches wanting to know how to start this type of a ministry, I authored *Woman to Woman Mentoring, How to Start, Grow, and Maintain A Mentoring Ministry DVD Leadership Kit* (LifeWay Press).

As I traveled throughout the United States and Canada, training and speaking on mentoring, I heard numerous requests for a Bible study depicting God's plan for mentors and mentees— "M&M'S,"as we fondly call them. One morning as my husband completed his quiet time with the Lord, Dave asked me if I had ever considered writing Bible studies based on mentoring relationships in the Bible. He knew that many M&M'S enjoy doing a Bible study together, and Dave felt that one focused on what God says about mentoring relationships would help answer many of the questions M&M'S pose.

After much prayer—and my husband's prodding—I decided to look in the Bible to see how many mentoring relationships I could find. Before long, I had discovered 12. This was my confirmation to begin writing the "Face-to-Face" Bible study series (formerly known as *Mentoring God's Way*). My passion and life mission is to help one generation of believers connect to the next generation and pass down God's plan for the Christian life. I trust that the "Face-to-Face" Bible study series will help you do exactly that.

What Is Mentoring?

I love Dee Brestin's depiction of the informality of mentoring in *The Friendships of Women Workbook*: "It's not to be a dependent relationship,

Face-to-Face with Mary and Martha

but simply a friendship as you spend time with a woman who is further down the road, at least in some areas of her Christian life. Win Couchman says, 'Mentoring works very nicely over a cup of coffee.'"

For those who like more concrete and specific definitions, *Roget's Super Thesaurus* provides this explanation of the root word of *mentoring*. It defines *mentor* as a teacher, guide, coach, or advisor. Most dictionaries define the word *mentor* as a trusted and wise counselor. To combine Dee's and the reference definitions with the Christian perspective: a Christian mentor is a spiritually mature woman who is a trusted and wise teacher, guide, coach, counselor, advisor, and friend. Thus, a *mentee* is someone willing to be taught, guided, coached, advised, or counseled by a trusted, wise, and spiritually older woman friend. Christian mentoring is sharing with another woman the many wonders you have seen God do in your life, and assuring her that He will do them in her life, too, as you both discover God's purpose and plan for your lives together.

Mentoring is not a hierarchy: it's always a two-way, mutually benefiting relationship where both participants learn from the other. Chris Tiegreen, author of my favorite devotional, *The One-Year Walk with God Devotional*, reminds us why it is always better to seek God's ways together:

> The Bible gives us solid wisdom on which to base our lives. But while it is absolute, its interpretation can vary widely. That's where advice comes in. Never underestimate the body of Christ. He has crafted us to live in community. Wisdom usually comes not to godly individuals but to godly fellowships. Are you seeking direction? Know your heart, but do not trust it entirely. Measure it by biblical wisdom and the counsel of those who follow it well.
> —Chris Tiegreen, *The One Year Walk With God Devotional*, June 27 devotional

The Bible also clearly instructs men to mentor men and women to mentor women. Titus 2:1–8 is the traditional "mentoring" passage:

> *You must teach what is in accord with sound doctrine. Teach the older men to be temperate, worthy of respect, self-controlled, and*

sound in faith, in love and in endurance. Likewise, teach the older women to be reverent in the way they live, not to be slanderers or addicted to much wine, but to teach what is good. Then they can train the younger women to love their husbands and children, to be self-controlled and pure, to be busy at home, to be kind, and to be subject to their husbands, so that no one will malign the word of God. Similarly, encourage the young men to be self-controlled. In everything set them an example by doing what is good. In your teaching show integrity, seriousness and soundness of speech that cannot be condemned, so that those who oppose you may be ashamed because they have nothing bad to say about us.

1 Peter 5:2–4 (NLT) could be addressing mentors:

Care for the flock that God has entrusted to you. Watch over it willingly, not grudgingly—not for what you will get out of it, but because you are eager to serve God. Don't lord it over the people assigned to your care, but lead them by your own good example. And when the Great Shepherd appears, you will receive a crown of never-ending glory and honor.

A mentor doesn't need to be an expert on the Bible or God, and she doesn't need to have a perfect life. If that were the case, none of us would qualify. A mentor simply needs to be willing to share her life experiences with another woman and be an example and role model of how a Christian woman does life. And how do we learn to be a godly role model? Answer: *"Remember your leaders who taught you the word of God. Think of all the good that has come from their lives, and follow the example of their faith"* (Hebrews 13:7 NLT).

Mentoring is not *doing* a ministry: It is *being* a godly woman who follows the Lord's command: *"One generation will commend your works to another; they will tell of your mighty acts"* (Psalm 145:4).

Face-to-Face with Mary and Martha

WHO ARE M&M'S?

In the Woman to Woman Mentoring Ministry, we lovingly refer to mentors and mentees as "M&M'S"—no, that's not the candy, although we always have M&M's® candy at our events. And just like the candy, there are varieties of M&M relationships—no two are the same. M&M'S may be—friends, acquaintances, family members, workers, neighbors, members of a mentoring or other ministry, team members, women with similar life experiences, or any two women—who want to grow spiritually together.

M&M'S AND MORE!

The "Face-to-Face" Bible study series has a variety of applications. You can enjoy this study:
- On your own
- As a mentor and mentee (M&M'S) in a mentoring or discipleship relationship
- Between two friends
- Between two relatives
- As a small or large group studying together
- As a churchwide Bible study

The Bible studies offer three types of questions:
- ON YOUR OWN: questions for doing the study individually
- M&M'S: questions for mentors and mentees, two friends, or relatives studying together
- ON YOUR OWN AND M&M'S: questions applicable to both individuals and those studying together
- GROUPS: answer all the questions, with a Leader's/Facilitator's Guide in each book.

STUDY FORMAT

There are five main "Sessions" comprised of five study days. Each day's study includes:
- Scriptures and questions for you to study and answer;
- Face-to-Face Reflections—a discussion of the day's topic;

- Personal Parable—a story depicting and applying the day's topic; and
- Mentoring Moment—takeaway wisdom for the day.

At the end of each Session there is:
- Faith in Action—an opportunity for life application of the lessons learned
- Let's Pray Together—a prayer for me to pray with you

Following Session Five are Closing Materials:
- Let's Pray a Closing Prayer Together
- Janet's Suggestions—ideas for further study
- Leader's Guide for Group-Study Facilitators and M&M'S
- Session Guide
- Prayer and Praise Journal

SUGGESTIONS FOR INDIVIDUAL STUDY

I admire you for seeking out this study on your own and having the desire and discipline to work on it by yourself. I like to grow in the knowledge of the Lord and His Word and have found that my most relevant insights from God come when I seek Him by myself in a quiet place. Have fun on your own, and share with someone all you are learning.

1. A good way to stay consistent in your studying is to work a little each day during your quiet time in the morning or evening.

2. Tell someone you have started this study and ask him or her to keep you accountable to completing it.

SUGGESTIONS FOR M&M'S—
MENTORS AND MENTEES, FRIENDS, AND RELATIVES

I hope the study of *Face-to-Face with Mary and Martha: Sisters in Christ* adds a new dimension to your M&M relationship. Here are a few study tips:

1. Come to your meetings prepared to discuss your answers to the session's questions.

2. Or you may decide to answer the questions together during your meetings.

3. If you don't live near each other, you can have phone or online discussions.

4. Remember, the questions are to enlighten and not divide; be honest and open, but also loving and kind.

SUGGESTIONS FOR GROUP STUDY

I love group studies because you get to hear other people's points of view and lasting friendships often develop. Your meetings should be fun, informative, relevant and applicable to group members' lives. Enjoy yourself with your fellow sisters in Christ, but remember that joining a group study *does* mean commitment. So please attend your scheduled meetings, unless there is a real emergency. I suggest the following courtesies:

1. Put the meeting dates on your calendar.

2. Commit to doing your study and come prepared to discuss it. This honors the rest of the group, and you will get so much more from the sessions.

3. Ask questions—because, chances are, someone else has the same question.

4. Participate in the discussion, but be cautious of dominating the conversation. For example, if you have answered several questions, even though you know all the answers, let someone else have a turn. Try to encourage a less outgoing member to share.

5. Listen when others speak and give each speaker your full attention.

6. Arrive on time.

7. Keep in confidence the information shared in the group.

LEADERS AND FACILITATORS

When I lead and facilitate Bible-study groups, I value a complete and detailed Leader's Guide, so that is what I have provided for you. The "Face-to-Face" Bible study series has a Leader's Guide at the end of each book, to provide the leader/facilitator with creative ideas for:

1. Guiding group discussion

2. Adding life application and variety to the sessions

3. Accommodating the varied learning styles of the group (visual learners, hands-on learners, auditory learners, and more)

TO YOU—THE READER

Whatever way you are doing this study, God has a message and a lesson just for you. Here are some suggestions I pray will enhance your experience studying *Face-to-Face with Mary and Martha*.

1. Start each session with prayer and ask the Lord to speak to you through the Scripture readings, the prayerful answering of the questions, and the interaction with others.

2. Set your own pace. I provide breaking points, but make it comfortable for yourself and break as you need to do so.

3. If you're not sure how to answer a question, move on; but continue praying and thinking about the answer. Often my answers come quickly, but God's answers are the most fruitful.

4. Unless otherwise indicated, all the questions relate to NIV Bible passages. Lists of Scripture are sequential, as they appear in

the Bible. You will be looking up Scripture references in your Bible, which is an invaluable way to study and learn about the Bible.

5. Use the space provided to answer questions, but don't feel obligated to fill the space. However, if you need more room, continue answering in a separate journal.

6. A book effectively used for study should be underlined, highlighted, and comments written in the margins, so interact with the material.

7. At the end of Session Five, you will find suggestions from me on books to read or activities to delve deeper into what God may be teaching you about the biblical M&M relationship featured in the study.

8. Use the Prayer and Praise Journal beginning on page 138 to record the mighty work God does in your life during this study. Journal prayer requests and note when God answers.

9. Have some chocolate. After reading about M&M'S throughout the study, you'll be ready for some candy!

My heart, admiration, and encouragement go out to you with this book. I pray that mentoring becomes a vital part of your life. The "Face-to-Face" Bible study series is another way the Lord allows me to "feed My sheep." And I hope that you will enjoy this and other "Face-to-Face" Bible studies and "feed" others as well.

About His Work,
Janet

THEIR STORY

CAN YOU RELATE?

—AMBERLY DAWN NEESE

As a busy author and speaker, I meet thousands of people a year. What initially caught my attention about Debbie was her daughter. I was speaking at a mother/daughter retreat at a camp in Southern California. At this camp, there was a wooden pole over 100 feet tall that daring campers often climbed to illustrate their bravery. One particular mom was running out of steam as she neared the top. The voice of her daughter sliced through the noise of the crowd, "You can do *all* things through Christ who gives you strength, Mom!" The scene brought tears to my eyes. As the mom reached the summit, as was custom, she yelled out a goal she had. She was too far away for any of us to decipher her words, but the experience impressed me greatly.

Three weeks later, I had a speaking engagement at a youth camp in Arizona. As I was greeting arriving campers, I recognized the face of the girl who had encouraged her mother weeks before. She excitedly introduced herself and her mother who was serving as a camp counselor. The mother, Debbie, and I hit it off immediately. Like me, she was a pastor's wife. Not unlike me, she struggled with the pressures therein. We talked all week and decided that both of us were in need of a prayer partner. Ignoring the fact that we did not live near each other, we vowed to call each other once a week and spend time in prayer for one another. Three years later, I still eagerly anticipate our weekly call. We share our struggles, our hearts, our triumphs, and our vulnerability. We know the other is a safe place for honesty with information shared only with the Father. Looking back, I can see God's hand in this relationship of accountability from its genesis. She is a "Mary"—one who worships and prays fervently, yet sometimes struggles to get things accomplished. I am a "Martha"—one who sometimes gets so caught up in accomplishing things I forget to seek the face of God. We challenge each other. I have learned a great deal from this godly woman, and thankfully, she has expressed that she has gleaned from me as well. I love her and praise God for this relationship.

Recently, she asked me if I heard her express her goal on the top of that pole years earlier. I admitted that I hadn't. She divulged that the words she shouted up to heaven were: "I need a friend, God. My goal is to find one."

Day One

How Does Mary and Martha's Story Relate to Us?

$\mathcal{M}$ary and Martha were sisters who, with their brother Lazarus, were good friends of Jesus.

On Your Own and M&M's

Q: Read the following passages and note thoughts you didn't previously notice about the story of Mary, Martha, and Lazarus and their relationship with Jesus.

- Luke 10:38–42

- John 11:1–48

- John 12:1–11

Q: Did you learn anything new that surprised you?

Q: What parts of the story do you relate to the most?

Most women who know the story of Mary and Martha say they want to be more of a Mary and less of a Martha: a challenging goal in a world that focuses on achievement, acquisition, and busyness. We have become a very materialistic, frantic, and isolated society. A common lament I hear from women is the one expressed in the opening story of Debbie and Amberly—loneliness. Women are searching for a Christian friend, and yet when given the opportunity to be in an M&M relationship or a friendship, they often respond with "Oh, I have no time for that. I'm too busy." It's a paradox that we don't allow ourselves to enjoy what our heart deeply desires—relationships. Friendships and M&M relationships do take time, but I am convinced that women would experience far less depression and illness if they allowed themselves to indulge in the blessings of a nurturing spiritual friendship.

Usually, we look at the story of Mary and Martha from the aspect of worship versus busyness, but there is so much more we can learn from what the Scriptures tell us about these two sisters—particularly, how their story applies to relationships.

* * *

Mentoring Moment

"The disciple of Jesus is not the deluxe or heavy-duty model
of the Christian—especially padded, textured, streamlined,
and empowered for the fast lane on the straight and narrow
way. He stands on the pages of the New Testament
as the first level of basic transportation in the kingdom of God."
—Dallas Willard, "Discipleship for Christians Today,"
Christianity Today

* * *

DAY TWO

CHRONOLOGICAL AGE
VERSUS SPIRITUAL AGE

*Y*ou might not know that Martha is the older sister since Mary appears to be the more spiritually sensitive and mature of the two. We learn in John 11:27 that Martha is a believer, but the first time we meet Martha in Luke 10:38–42, she doesn't seem to understand the deity of Jesus, while her younger sister, Mary, immediately discerns and recognizes the significance of Jesus's visit.

ON YOUR OWN AND M&M'S

Q: Reread "What is Mentoring?" on page 8 and "Who Are M&M'S?" on page 11.

Q: Read Titus 2:1–8. How do the verses apply to mentoring and M&M'S?

● We often assume this passage refers strictly to chronological age, but reread Titus 2:1–8 inserting the word *spiritually* in front of the words *older* and *younger*. What interpretation does that give these verses?

Q: How does the story of Mary and Martha suggest that a chronologically older woman is not always equipped or ready to mentor?

Q: Underline the words *teach* and *train* in Titus 2:1–8 in your Bible.

Q: What has a spiritually older woman taught you about God that you could teach to a woman spiritually younger than you, regardless of your chronological ages?

Q: How might the chronological age difference between Mary and Martha (Martha being the older sister) have influenced the roles they each took in Luke 10:38–42?

Q: How might their spiritual age difference have influenced their actions?

M & M'S

Q: Is the "spiritually older woman" chronologically older or younger in your relationship?

Q: If she is younger in age, does that make either of you uncomfortable? If so, take time at your next meeting to discuss any concerns you still have. Make some notes here:

Q: If both of you are the same spiritual and chronological age, how can you apply this biblical truth: *"As iron sharpens iron, so a friend sharpens a friend"* (Proverbs 27:17 NLT)?

Spiritual age doesn't necessarily parallel chronological age. Accepting Christ as our Savior or choosing to mature in our walk with Him is a personal choice that can occur at any age. In some families, the person closest to Jesus is a small child.

Titus was a young pastor starting a church plant in the exceedingly pagan city of Crete. Just like in today's churches, the first believers joining Titus's church were not all elderly: they varied in age and became the first generation of believers in his church. As more people of all ages joined the church, Paul tells Titus in verses 2:1–8 that he should have the first generation of *spiritually* older men and women teach and train the next generation of *spiritually* younger men and women: men teaching men and women teaching women.

Traditionally, we look at Titus 2:3–5 as instructing only chronologically older women to teach and train chronologically younger women. But many women accept Christ later in life, and even though they are wise in the world, they are babies in the Lord—older women in worldly years, but younger in spiritual years. These *spiritually younger* women need a *spiritually older* mentor, who just might be the same chronological age, or even younger.

If you accepted Christ at a young age, you are older in the Lord than someone who accepted Christ as an adult—you are the "Titus 2 older woman" whom God has called to teach and train what you have learned about the Christian life to spiritually younger women He puts in your path.

M&M'S can be friends, relatives, acquaintances, coworkers—any two women who want to learn and grow together in Christ.

PERSONAL PARABLE

In my own family, my daughter-in-law, Janel, is younger in age than my daughter Kim, but Janel has been a Christian since childhood and Kim became a Christian at age 25. Janel married and became a mom before Kim had those life experiences. Even though Janel is chronologically younger than Kim is, Janel is spiritually and experientially older and is a role model and mentor to Kim, who often says: "Mom, Janel is so wise. I love to hear her perspective on things!"

While theirs is not a formal mentoring relationship, Kim watches, asks questions, and considers Janel to be a wise and trusted counsel—so as sisters-in-law, Janel indeed is mentoring Kim.

Mentoring Moment

Mentoring is simply teaching to another woman what someone has taught you, so she can teach another woman what you taught her, so she can teach another woman … and on the training goes down through the generations, regardless of how many birthdays any of you have had. It's sharing with another woman the things you have seen God do in your life.

Day Three

Celebrating Your Spiritual Birthday

Everyone loves a birthday party. My toddler grand-daughter, Katelyn, calls funnels, measuring cups, cones—anything that looks like a birthday hat—a "happy hat." However, as we age, we may dread another birthday, but we should always put on our happy hats and joyously celebrate our spiritual birthday.

On Your Own and M&M's

Q: Read John 11:25. Jesus is asking Martha if she is a believer. Another term for becoming a believer is being "born again." Read John 3:3–7. Why do we need to be a "born-again" believer?

Q: Psalm 145:4–7 is one of my favorite passages to describe mentoring. Look for the verbs in these verses and describe what one generation of believers is to do for the next generation.

Q: How does your being willing to share with someone the things you have seen God do in your life help to grow the other person's faith?

Q: How does sharing your testimony grow your own faith?

ON YOUR OWN

Q: If you have accepted Christ into your heart as your personal savior and are "born again," describe the circumstances and the date (as close as you can remember) of your rebirth in Christ. This is your spiritual birthday.

Q: If you haven't yet made a decision to trust in Christ for eternal life and to follow Him, what is holding you back?

Q: Seek out a Christian you admire and ask if she can either answer your questions or direct you to someone who can. Or if you are ready right now, pray the Salvation Prayer on page 28 and then seek out a mentor to disciple you or enroll in your church's discipleship class.

M & M'S

Q: Early in your relationship, share with each other your testimony of becoming a Christian and have dessert together to celebrate your spiritual birthdays.

Q: If you are the mentee and haven't accepted Jesus as your personal Savior, talk about your hesitations with your mentor

Q: Mentor, help your mentee find answers to her spiritual questions. That's one of the reasons God has put the two of you together.

Q: Mentee, if you are ready to ask Jesus into your heart, pray this Salvation Prayer.

SALVATION PRAYER

Jesus, I know that I am a sinner and have not led a life completely pleasing to You. I am so sorry for the sins I have committed in the past, and I ask for Your forgiveness and help in not sinning in the future. I do believe that You, Jesus, are the Son of God, and that You died to pay the price for my sins, and then You rose in three days so that I could have eternal life. From this day forward I give my life to You, Jesus, and I ask You to reside in my heart and guide my life. In Jesus's name, I pray. Amen.

If you just prayed that prayer: Welcome to the family of God! Today is your spiritual birthday: you are born again! Celebrate and tell others about the decision you just made to become a follower of Jesus Christ—this is your testimony. Now you are ready to grow and mature spiritually, and this study will have so much more meaning to you. You go, girl!

FACE-TO-FACE REFLECTIONS

God wants us to share our "born again" testimony because it does two things: One, it encourages others and may actually help him or her make a decision for Christ; secondly, it strengthens our own faith when we continuously remind ourselves of how Jesus changed our life. One of the first things a new believer should do is tell someone about making a decision for Christ. If you found the cure for cancer, you would shout it from the rooftops. Well, you have found something better: the cure for death—eternal life.

PERSONAL PARABLE

When I speak, I always share my "feed My sheep" testimony sharing how I rededicated my life to Christ at a Harvest Crusade and answered His call to go into full-time ministry (page 8). I have written this testimony in most of my books, and I never tire of telling it because I love recounting the story of the incredible work God has done in my life and ministry. One day my friend, Jane, commented that my testimony always sounds the same. My response to her was she should worry if it ever changed because then I would be making up a story. Nothing could enhance the miraculous reality of God changing my life. I have told my testimony hundreds of times, and it's always fresh and new both to my listener and to me.

Mentoring Moment

In your hearts set apart Christ as Lord.
Always be prepared to give an answer to everyone
who asks you to give the reason for the hope that you have.
But do this with gentleness and respect.
— 1 Peter 3:15

DAY FOUR

SISTER TO SISTER

Mary and Martha were biological sisters. Sometimes we say harsh or discourteous words to relatives that we would never say to someone outside our family.

ON YOUR OWN AND M&M'S

Q: Describe the scene in Luke 10:38–42.

Q: Describe a time when a similar scene took place in your home.

- If you were part of the conflict, were you a Mary or a Martha?

- If you were a Martha, how have you learned to handle situations differently as you mature in your Christian life?

Q: Why do you think we are not as kind, considerate, and patient with family members as we are with strangers?

Q: John 11:32 is the only recorded comment of Mary, yet her actions tell us so much about the way she served and worshipped the Lord. Look up the following verses and note what the Bible says about a quiet, gracious, and gentle spirit.

- Amos 5:13a

- Galatians 5:22–23

- Colossians 4:6

- 1 Thessalonians 4:11

- 1 Timothy 2:1–3

- 1 Peter 3:3–5

FACE-TO-FACE REFLECTIONS

Martha is very irritated and critical of her younger sister. It almost seems like they have experienced this scenario before in their house. Martha, the bossy older sister, is trying to get the younger Mary to conform to Martha's schedule and way of doing things. Mary is oblivious. She sits mesmerized at Jesus's feet, paying no attention to Martha's huffing, sighing, and fretting. This makes Martha even madder. Martha actually scolds Mary in front of everyone and asks their honored guest, Jesus, to side with her in reprimanding Mary for being lazy and not helping her.

Interestingly, Mary doesn't try to defend herself or call on Jesus to stand up for her. She has just been humiliated and verbally attacked in front of their guests, but Mary remains calm. She doesn't add to the unpleasantness or play favorites with Jesus by extending an "I-told-you-so ha-ha" look or comment to Martha when Jesus reprimands her. Mary keeps a quiet and gentle spirit through it all.

Much role modeling takes place in the home. Depending on how an older sister chooses to live her life, she can be a good or bad role model for younger siblings. A younger sister often looks up to an older sister and learns from the experiences and life circumstances she sees her older sister encountering; or she can resent her older sister getting to do things sooner and having more freedom in the family.

The older sister may see the younger sister as impressionable and requiring nurturing and guidance; or she may see her as a pesky, nuisance "kid sister." Many of us outgrow childish ways of reacting to siblings, and then others are still feuding and fighting into old age.

PERSONAL PARABLE

Of course, not all sisters have difficult relationships. I once led a women's Bible study where one of the ladies in the group eagerly invited her younger sister to join us. I was thrilled, and even more impressed, to learn that there was a ten-year age difference between the sisters! They resembled Mary and Martha since the older sister is a very busy, energetic, working mother of three, and the younger sister is a quieter, calmer stay-at-home mom. These two sisters easily might live in different worlds, but they chose to enjoy a loving, peaceful, spiritually growing relationship.

* * *

Mentoring Moment

The way we *speak* influences the way we *treat* others.

* * *

Face-to-Face with Mary and Martha

DAY FIVE

SISTERS IN CHRIST

*I*n spite of the scene in Luke 10:38–42, Mary and Martha were very much a part of each other's lives, and perhaps were friends as well as sisters: the Scriptures always mention them together. Like Mary and Martha and the sisters in my Bible study, sisters who share a family heritage often remain close throughout life. However, sisters also can go separate ways as adults. But sisters in Christ have a spiritual heritage that is often stronger than blood ties.

ON YOUR OWN AND M&M'S

Q: If you don't have a sister or a close relationship with your sister, is there anyone who is like a sister to you?

Q: Proverbs 18:24 (personalized) reads: *"There is a friend who sticks closer than a [sister]."* Do you have a close friend like that? If so, where did you meet her? If not, how could you develop such a sisterly friendship?

Q: What does the term *sisters in Christ* mean to you?

Q: What other types of "sisters" do you have in your life? (Think "sisterhood.")

Q: Now think about your experiences with sisters in Christ. Have you had a "Mary and Martha" (Luke 10:38–42) encounter with another Christian sister, maybe working on a committee or serving in the church? Without using names, describe what happened.

● What role did you play?

● If you are not pleased with how you handled the situation, what can you learn from Jesus's words to Martha in Luke 10:41–42?

Q: Read Galatians 6:10 and 1 Thessalonians 2:7–8, 11. How will you implement these passages to be a sister in Christ to a blood relative, Christian, or sisterhood sister?

Q: Who do you know who needs a hug, a phone call, a note, an invitation to your Bible study, or to know Jesus better (fill in the blank)? _____ Commit now to contact her this week.

M & M'S

Q: If you are sisters, sisters in Christ, friends, or any combination, how do your relationship dynamics compare to Mary's and Martha's relationship?

Q: What steps can you take to enhance your relationship?

FACE-TO-FACE REFLECTIONS

A sisterhood often develops among women who have been on a similar life journey. For example, I am a breast cancer survivor, and I had the opportunity to write a book for my "breast cancer sisters" to mentor them from my experience and the experience of other breast cancer sisters. In my book, *Dear God, They Say It's Cancer: A Companion Guide for Women on the Breast Cancer Journey*, every chapter has a section titled "A Sister Shares" in which another woman with breast cancer shares her story. I actually have an entire chapter titled "Breast Cancer Sisters." Here is a quote from my "Dear God" journal entry in that chapter:

> Dear God, help me always remember every breast cancer woman is my sister, regardless of her position or state in life, no matter how young or old, famous or unknown, rich or poor. This is a sisterhood not of our choosing.

PERSONAL PARABLE

I tell a cute story about Jane, my friend and sister in Christ. Jane was a new Christian when she joined the Saddleback Woman to Woman Mentoring Ministry, and she told us her family was Dutch. That surprised me because Jane has dark hair, olive complexion, and brown eyes. I expected Dutch heritage to result in fair skin, blond hair, and blue eyes. One day Jane announced that she was going to our church's women's retreat with her *"real* sister!" She put such an emphasis on the word *real*, I thought: That makes sense. Jane must be adopted, and she has located her real blood sister. That's why she doesn't look Dutch.

Later, I was over at Jane's house and saw a family picture. "Wow!" I said. "You fit in so perfectly. You actually look like the rest of your family!" Jane replied, "Of course, I look like them. This *is* my family." I responded, "I know, but you're adopted, and it's so amazing that they made such a great match!"

Between gales of laughter, Jane asked why I thought she was adopted. I explained my assumption based on her comment about taking her *real* sister to the retreat, and the fact that she doesn't look Dutch. Jane assured me she wasn't adopted and her family is Indonesian Dutch, which explains the dark skin and features. Still wiping the laughing tears from her eyes, Jane said she emphasized "*real* sister" to differentiate from her sisters in Christ!

We still get a good laugh about that. As a new Christian, Jane was thrilled to know she now had a new family with many sisters—she actually was adopted into the family of God.

Mentoring Moment

Friends from the start, sisters to the end:
that's the definition of a true best friend.

FAITH IN ACTION

What one thing from this session does God want you to apply in your life today?

LET'S PRAY TOGETHER

Lord, help us be receptive to the ways You want to use our life experiences to help and guide others to a closer walk with You. Let us remember that mentoring is simply being a role model and sharing our life with another woman, regardless of age. Help us learn from others and be aware of those who could learn from us. Show us how to love our sisters and sisters in Christ the way You love them. Amen.

WE ARE WONDERFULLY
MADE-DIFFERENT

Day One

Complementary Personalities

*I*f you have ever taken a personality test, you know how revealing they can be. You discover that many of the character qualities you admire most in yourself are actually annoying to others. Every personality type has a positive and negative side, and we usually strive to "accentuate the positive and eliminate the negative." The problem is that we don't always see ourselves as others see us. What we might think is our most positive quality could be the very thing that irritates everyone around us.

Two of my favorite personality specialists, Florence Littauer and Gary Smalley, categorize four personality types, which Smalley relates to animal traits.

The Popular Sanguine/Otter—the life of the party—is outgoing, social, emotional, colorful, extroverted, and loves to have a good time. Sanguines are demonstrative, enthusiastic, expressive, curious, wide-eyed, innocent, live in the present, sincere at heart, and often childlike—their focus is fun! But they can be so busy having fun that they lose track of time, thus missing appointments, or continually running late. Their happy-go-lucky and free-spirit attitude often labels them "flaky" and inconsiderate.

The Powerful Choleric/Lion—the leader—is also an extrovert, but that's the only similarity to a Sanguine. Cholerics take charge, get things done efficiently, stay focused, and don't get distracted. Strong-willed, decisive, and independent bottom-line achievers, they are not afraid of hard work and must correct wrongs. Being goal-oriented, they seek practical solutions, move quickly to action, delegate work, insist on production, and thrive on opposition. But often they come across as stern, bossy, unfeeling, and lacking in compassion and finesse.

The Peaceful Phlegmatic/Golden Retriever—the peacemaker—gets along with everyone. Even-tempered, patient, introverted Phlegmatics seldom lose their cool and willingly defer the floor to others to avoid conflict at any cost. They are calm, cool, consistent, sympathetic, kind, easygoing, relaxed, behind-the-scenes team players. Not wanting to offend anyone, Phlegmatics remain neutral and indecisive, but this can be their most offensive trait interpreted as wishy-washy, noncommittal procrastination.

The Perfect Melancholy/Beaver—the thinker—is an introvert with a great deal of compassion for others. They are analytical, detailed, manual and instruction reader perfectionists. Melancholies are conscientious, serious, self-sacrificing, purposeful idealists, who are deep, thoughtful, and sensitive. But sensitivity and striving to reach perfection often leaves them depressed with many unfinished tasks. Analyzing everything can come across as negative and pessimistic.

ON YOUR OWN AND M&M'S

Q: Based on the above discussion of personalities, and the actions and reactions of Mary and Martha in the scenarios described in the Luke and John passages you read earlier, which personality type would you say Mary is and why?

Q: Which personality type do you think Martha is and why?

Q: What positive and negative personality traits do Mary and Martha each display?

Q: Do you know your personality type? If so, what are you?

- If not, can you make a guess from the above descriptions? (If you have never taken a personality test, see Janet's Suggestions, page 122–123.)
- What positive and negative traits of your personality do you often display?

- What could you change to maximize the positive and minimize the negative?

Q: We usually believe our way is the "right way." What does the Bible caution about this attitude?
- Proverbs 14:12
- Proverbs 16:2
- Proverbs 18:17

Q: How does your personality type affect your interactions with others?

- Your relationship with God?

- Your ministry?

M & M'S

Q: How might each of your personality types affect:
- Your communication with each other?

- Setting goals for your relationship and working at them together?

Q: If you are opposite personalities, how can you balance each other's temperament?

Q: If you are similar personalities, how has that affected your relationship?

Q: How does knowing your personality differences help you extend grace to each other?

FACE-TO-FACE REFLECTIONS

It's important to remember that we are all God's unique creation and there is no right or wrong personality. All individuals have a combination of personality characteristics, but we usually possess one dominant personality type, with a close second, and then little bits of the other two. Mary and Martha are strikingly different personalities, and we see the perceived good and offensive sides of each one's personality traits. In Luke 10:38–42, Martha certainly thought her request was justified, but Jesus pointed out to her that it was not. What a shock.

Max Lucado discusses Mary and Martha in his book, *He Still Moves Stones*:

> It's the story of Martha. A dear soul given to hospitality and organization. More frugal than frivolous, more practical than pensive, her household is a tight ship and she is a stern captain. Ask her to choose between a book and a broom, and she'll take the broom.
>
> Mary, however, will take the book. Mary is Martha's sister. Same parents, different priorities. Martha has things to do. Mary has thoughts to think. The dishes can wait. Let Martha go to the market; Mary will go to the library.
>
> Two sisters. Two personalities. And as long as they understand each other, it's hand in glove. But when the one resents the other, it's flint and stone.

We will see later how Mary and Martha worked on achieving a personality balance in their ministry together. In Sue and Larry Richardson's book, *Every Woman in the Bible*, they point out that:

"While the two sisters had distinctly different personalities, they were usually together when mentioned in Scripture."

Mentoring Moment

"Mary was the sunlight to Martha's thunder. She was the caboose to Martha's locomotive. Mary's bent was to meander through life, pausing to smell the roses. Martha was more likely to pick the roses, quickly cut the stems at an angle, and arrange them in a vase with baby's breath and ferns. That is not to say one is right and one is wrong. We are all different, and that is just how God made us. Each gifting and personality has its own strengths and weaknesses, its glories and temptations."
—Joanna Weaver, *Having a Mary Heart in a Martha World*

Day Two

Using Our Spiritual Gifts

*J*ust as God created us with diverse personality traits, He also gave us different spiritual gifts. The challenge becomes learning to use our personality and spiritual gifts to the glory of God and not letting our differences divide us.

On Your Own and M&M's

Q: Read each of the following verses that discuss spiritual gifts and then answer the questions that follow:
- Romans 12:3–8
- 1 Corinthians 7:7
- 1 Corinthians 12:1–12, 27–31
- 1 Peter 4:10–11

  - What are some spiritual gifts?

  - Who gives spiritual gifts?

  - When do we receive our spiritual gift or gifts?

  - Why doesn't everyone receive the same gift?

- How are we to use our spiritual gifts?

- What is the purpose of spiritual gifts?

Q: Read 1 Corinthians 12:13–26. Why isn't one spiritual gift better than another?

Q: What spiritual gifts do you see in Mary?

Q: Traditionally, a body was anointed *after* death by pouring oil over the head, but Mary anointed Jesus *before* His death and anointed both His head and feet (Matthew 26:6–9 and John 12:1–3). Read Psalm 16:10 and Acts 2:22–28. What do these Scriptures reveal about Jesus's death?

- What insight and spiritual gifts did Mary display by anointing Jesus while He was still alive?

- Where and when do you think Mary gleaned this insight (Luke 10:39)?

- Mary seemed to be the only one who understood that Jesus was going to die. What was everyone else's reaction to Mary's gesture (Matthew 26:8–9 and John 12:4–5)?

Q: What spiritual gifts do you see in Martha?

Q: What do these verses say about the spiritual gift of hospitality?
- Romans 12:9–13
- Romans 16:23
- 1 Peter 4:9

Q: Now look again at Martha's actions in Luke 10:38–42. How could she have been more hospitable?

● What would the revised scene look like, starting with Jesus coming to the front door?

Q: What spiritual gifts do you have? If you have never taken a spiritual gifts test, look at Janet's Suggestions on page 122.

M & M'S

Q: How could you combine your spiritual gifts to do ministry or a project together?

FACE-TO-FACE REFLECTIONS

In the *compassionate* anointing of Jesus's feet, Mary displayed numerous spiritual gifts, which I have highlighted in this discussion. Only the lowliest *humble* servants attended to guests' dirty, smelly feet. Using her hair to dry His feet required *fearless faith* and *tenacity* because "respectable women" in that day never wore their hair unbound in public. Anointing Jesus before His death revealed *discernment* and *wisdom*: she knew not only that He was soon to die, but also it might suggest that He would not need the traditional anointing after death because His body was not going to decay. Judas said the monetary value of the oil Mary used for anointing was worth a year's wages: Mary *gave selflessly* of herself and her possessions. And perhaps the oil was "family oil," which Martha also *freely gave*.

Martha also displayed the gifts of *leadership* and *service*. She apparently planned, organized, prepared, and served the meals, and it seems was the overseer of the home. You might have initially said that Martha had the gift of *hospitality*. Originally, I thought that, too, before reading C. Peter Wagner's definition in his *Finding Your Spiritual Gifts* Questionnaire: "The special ability that God gives to certain members of the body of Christ to provide an open house and a warm welcome to those in need of food and lodging." Martha opened her house, but the warmth was lacking.

* * *

Mentoring Moment

"Spiritual gifts are no proof of spirituality."
—Samuel Chadwick

* * *

DAY THREE

UNIQUELY YOU FOR GOD'S GLORY

A t Saddleback Church, we refer to our SHAPE: S-piritual gifts H-eart A-bilities P-ersonality E-xperiences. Our pastor, Rick Warren, author of *The Purpose Driven Church*, says if we discover our SHAPE, life is much less stressful and serving the Lord will be a natural part of our purpose in life.

ON YOUR OWN AND M&M'S

Q: Mary seemed to know her purpose and SHAPE. She enjoyed the spiritual gifts of wisdom and discernment bathed in humility, mercy, and giving, and she used her personality and spiritual gifts to God's glory. For most of us, it is difficult to discern without critically judging. However, note what the Bible says about *discerning* and *judging* in the following Scriptures:

- Psalm 50:4
- Psalm 119:125
- Proverbs 3:21
- Proverbs 16:21
- John 7:24
- 1 Corinthians 4:3–5
- Philippians 1:9–11

Q: For a deeper study, look up the words *discern, discerning, judge* and *judgment* in a Bible concordance and study the indicated Scriptures. Learning to look in the Bible for answers to life's questions is vital to our spiritual growth. Note what you discover:

Q: Martha may have been operating out of her SHAPE when she took on the role of preparing food for guests. Earlier we said that Martha's personality and gifts were leadership—being the boss. Leaders usually delegate: they organize an event, but don't perform the tasks.

● How might Martha have better used her SHAPE to glorify God?

Q: How are you using your SHAPE—Heart, Abilities, Personality, and Experiences—to glorify God?

● Or like Martha, are you operating out of your SHAPE?

● What could you change to get more in SHAPE?

Q: Let Psalm 115:1 be your guide as you learn to use your gifts and talents for God's glory.

M & M'S

Q: How has God shaped each of you to serve?

Q: Mentor, provide guidance for your mentee in developing and maturing her SHAPE.

Q: How might God use your combined SHAPE for His glory?

I've been in leadership roles most of my life. I'm a visionary who sees the big picture, but as most leaders, I don't like dealing with details. Like Martha, my focus is on a successful outcome, which usually takes the help of others. The key to recruiting committed helpers is learning Mary's wisdom, discernment, and compassion; knowing what will make people want to help because they feel cared for and part of the plan, not just workers on a project.

When I left the business world and went into full-time ministry, I learned the term *servant leadership*. To be a good leader for Christ, I had to serve others and not expect them to serve me. I modified my SHAPE by working on the "H-eart," which meant being less judgmental and becoming more compassionate. Finding our SHAPE is always a work in progress.

PERSONAL PARABLE

You probably have experienced an invitation to someone's home for dinner where you could not wait to leave. The uptight, frazzled hostess was yelling at the kids, the dog, and her husband. She stayed in the kitchen, leaving you to entertain yourselves. When you finally sat down to eat, uncomfortable tension shrouded the table. Your hostess opened her home and prepared a meal, but a warm fellowship was gravely missing. She was out of her SHAPE.

I've been that hostess myself at times, and it was no fun. I loved having people over but always wanted to do something unique and different that cost too much time, energy, and money. I wore myself out thinking the house, the food, and the table needed to be perfect. I expected my husband and family to help and share my stress and exhaustion. When they chose not to participate in my craziness, or didn't know how to help in the "right way," I became even more upset and tense. While we covered it well during our guests' visit, none of us enjoyed the time as much as we could or should have.

As I mature, I realize that the emphasis should be on the people coming to share fellowship, food, and fun with us. It was prideful to want attention and praise for the extravagant meal I had prepared. I was actually putting the focus on me and not our guests. I think Martha learned this lesson the same way I did—from the words of Jesus.

* * *

Mentoring Moment

"Our God loves variety...
He has not distributed His gifts with absolute equity....
Everyone is accountable for the resources
he or she has been entrusted with. No more, no less.
The distribution is determined by the wisdom of God.
Spiritual maturity is not found in having all gifts or
defending all causes. It is found in accepting the diversity
of God's people and working within it."
—Chris Tiegreen, *The One Year Walk With God Devotional,*
June 26 devotional

* * *

DAY FOUR

MAKING BETTER CHOICES

*I*n her book, *Having a Mary Heart in a Martha World*, Joanna Weaver contrasts the "living room intimacy" of Mary with the "kitchen service" of Martha. You can't be joyful serving God in the kitchen—or wherever you are called to serve—if you haven't intimately met Jesus in the living room—or wherever you spend time with God.

ON YOUR OWN AND M&M'S

Q: Read how *The Message* describes the scene in Luke 10:38–40:

As they continued their travel, Jesus entered a village. A woman by the name of Martha welcomed him and made him feel quite at home. She had a sister, Mary, who sat before the Master, hanging on every word he said. But all she had to do in the kitchen pulled Martha away. Later, she stepped in, interrupting them. "Master, don't you care that my sister has abandoned the kitchen to me? Tell her to lend me a hand."

- How did Martha initially greet Jesus?

- What happened between the front door, the living room, and the kitchen?

Q: Looking again at Luke 10:38–40, when Mary and Martha's guests arrive:

- Where did Mary *first* spend her time?

- Where did Martha *first* spend her time?

- What distracted Martha away from Jesus in the living room?

- What distracts you from your "living room" time with Jesus?

Q: The New Revised Standard Version Bible translates Luke 10:42: *"There is need of only one thing. Mary has chosen the better part, which will not be taken away from her."*

- What is the "better part"?

- Why couldn't the "better part" be taken away from Mary?

- Jesus says the "better part" is a *choice*, indicating options. If Mary chose the "better part," what are the "worse part" or alternate choices?

Q: What steps have you taken to choose the "better part"—and what can wait?

- If you still have difficulty making that distinction, admit your struggle, pray, and commit to working on it. What is going to be your first step toward making better choices?

Q: What can you learn from Martha about your service for the Lord when you haven't spent enough time with Jesus?

Q: How will you make time to do this study?

Face-to-Face with Mary and Martha

M & M'S

Q: How will you make time for your relationship and working on this study together?

FACE-TO-FACE REFLECTIONS

We see Mary choosing to stay in the living room learning and listening at Jesus's feet before she had a heart that was ready to serve Him. Martha started out in the living room welcoming Jesus and the disciples into her home (Luke 10:38), but then she had a choice: *deity* or *duty*? Even though Mary's temperament probably made the choice easier for her, and Jesus knew exactly how God created Martha, Jesus still indicated Martha had a choice. And so do we. Just like Martha, if we let distractions pull us away from the feet of Jesus before our heart is ready to serve, all the wonderful work we "do for the Lord" potentially will be lost: it's the wrong choice.

Our perspective on entertaining changes as we first spend time with Jesus and learn what He thinks is important when we invite guests into our Christian homes. We learn that our guests must first see and feel Jesus and His love, peace, and tranquility: then everyone feels as if he or she were sitting at the feet of Jesus.

PERSONAL PARABLE

Several years ago at Christmas, we were having a family dinner the night before some of our children and grand-children returned to their distant homes. I carefully planned a simple dinner so I wouldn't be cooking instead of visiting. However, after dinner while cleaning up dishes in the kitchen, I heard sounds of joy coming from the living room. The adults were laughing and the grandbabies squealing with delight. Peeking around the corner of the kitchen, I saw the entire family gathered in the living room playing with the new basketball hoop we had given little Jacob for Christmas. The adults were throwing the ball from all corners of the living room, and the grandchildren stood under the hoop to catch the ball and run it to the next person to throw. As I stared at the sink full of dishes and made a mental note to do paper plates next time, I thought, *I should be out there playing or taking pictures, but I'll just wash a couple more things* ... Then Jesus took hold of my hands and heart. He said, "*Tomorrow your grandbabies leave, and your house will be quiet and still ... no laughter and play like tonight, and there will be plenty of time then for your tears to wash off these dishes.*" Heeding Jesus's gentle reprimand, I put the dish towel down, took off my apron, left the kitchen, and picked up the camera to catch the fun in the living room.

Mentoring Moment

Martha's excuse was duty—cleaning and cooking to do—she was a busy woman with people to feed and a table to set; she didn't have time to sit at Jesus's feet. Maybe our excuse is work, children, gym, hobbies, cooking, shopping, ministry work, laziness—whatever the reason we don't spend regular time with Jesus—it's a sin. Joanna Weaver points out: "The very *definition* of sin is separation from God. So no matter how important the activity, no matter how good it seems, if I use it as an excuse to hold God at arm's length, it is sin."

DAY FIVE

LEARNING FROM OUR MISTAKES

W e often characterize poor Martha by the first dinner party, failing to notice she was receptive to Jesus's admonishment to look at her sister Mary, who was the example and model of what Jesus valued most — spending time with Him. Martha responded and changed.

ON YOUR OWN AND M&M'S

Q: Contrast the dinner preparation in Luke 10:38–42 with the next time we see Jesus having dinner with Mary and Martha in John 12:1–8. What is different here?

Q: What do you think Martha learned between the two dinners?

- How do you think she learned it?

Q: Describe the atmosphere at the second dinner:

Q: Read Proverbs 17:1. What does this verse say to you?

Q: Read Acts 16:13–15 and Hebrews 13:1–2. What blessings have you experienced by opening up your house for use by God?

- Your life for use by God?

Q: What blessings might you have missed by not opening up your home?

- Your life?

Q: What changes will you make to choose the "better part" consistently?

Q: Why do you think I *chose* to start the Woman to Woman Mentoring Ministry in my home and now I train churches to do likewise?

M & M'S

Q: Share with each other ways you learned to prevent the stressful atmosphere that "being a Martha" can create in your life and home.

Q: Mentor, offer tips you have learned to help make entertaining easier and less stressful.

FACE-TO-FACE REFLECTIONS

Jesus and the guests in Luke 10:38–42 needed feeding, and Martha did the right thing by preparing a meal. But was the meal too extravagant and did she spend too much time getting the house in order? I once heard a woman say that she could never understand why her mom cleaned out cupboards when company was coming for dinner!

Perhaps Mary initially helped Martha, but then when the guests arrived she went out to visit with Jesus, leaving Martha to finish in the kitchen alone. Learning from this experience, maybe Martha decided the next dinner for Jesus would be a simple soup, bread, cheese and fruit she could prepare quickly, or in advance, rather than a roast with all the trimmings, salad, special dessert, and their mother's secret dipping sauce that took hours to prepare and used every dish in the house. Today, ordering pizza, fixing a salad, and dishing up ice cream with cookies for dessert feeds your guests, while allowing you time to enjoy them.

PERSONAL PARABLE

When I first started the Woman to Woman Mentoring Ministry, I knew our M&M Orientation Coffees should be in a home. Christian homes are safe, nurturing, loving environments where women feel comfortable getting to know each other. But I was hesitant to open up my home. Our couch was old and wallpaper was peeling off the guest bathroom wall: all improvements I was putting off until our last child left home. As I prayed about my hesitation, the Lord reminded me these women were coming to my home to meet each other and Him, not to do a *"House Beautiful"* tour. Jesus gave me a picture of the ladies in their colorful clothes sitting on my couch and their beauty covered the faded upholstery. The bathroom functioned—that's good enough. The Lord was challenging me to make the better choice. I am so glad I did.

What might have happened if I hadn't followed God's prompting to invite ladies into my home in spite of its imperfections? I don't know the answer, because I didn't wait. The time was right and God birthed the Woman to Woman Mentoring Ministry in my living room on that old couch. What I thought was unworthy, God made into something beautiful. I might not be sharing with you the blessings I learned about mentoring if I had waited until my house met my standards. Many women actually told me they felt Jesus in our home the minute they walked through the front door. It can't get any better than that!

Mentoring Moment

This lesson is much more effective if you can actually apply it. Plan an event in your home. (For M&M'S, maybe a dinner party for your families to meet would be fun). Prepare a survey and ask the guests to critique your hospitality. Let them know you want their honest evaluation so you can learn how to improve on making your guests feel comfortable and welcome.

FAITH IN ACTION

What one thing from this session does God want you to apply in your life today?

LET'S PRAY TOGETHER

Lord, help us learn to celebrate our differences. Give us wisdom to make wise choices and to recognize the "better part" is whatever gives us more time with You. Help us learn from our mistakes and take time to hear Your voice. Amen.

FIRST THINGS FIRST

DAY ONE

SETTING PRIORITIES

*T*he Lord is coming to dinner and bringing guests! You had your day all planned, but now you must prepare for your Royal Guest and His friends. Oh my goodness, where do you begin? What should you do first? Then what?

ON YOUR OWN AND M&M'S

Q: How do you think Martha answered these questions?

Q: How do you think Mary answered these questions?

Q: How would you answer these questions?

Q: How does Jesus answer these questions in Matthew 6:31–34?

Q: Read Matthew 22:37–40, the Great Commandment.
● How do you see Mary applying these verses?

- How did Martha have these verses reversed?

- How do you apply these verses to your life?

Q: Read John 1:1. How does this verse impress you with the importance of spending time with Jesus, reading your Bible and praying?

Q: What steps can you take to put Jesus first in your life, your work, and the work you do for Him?

M & M'S

Q: Your M&M is a very important person in your life. How are you doing at reprioritizing your life and schedule to make time for this relationship?
- Or are you always frenzied wondering how you can fit in time to do the study and meet with your M&M?

Q: Discuss the value you place on your time together and ways each of you have adjusted your schedule to make time to meet. Make notes here:

FACE-TO-FACE REFLECTIONS

When you enter into any type of a relationship, you must be willing to make time for it and give it a place of priority in your life. Like most of us, you probably have a very full life and calendar. You will need to pray about what to rearrange or remove from your current activities in order to create space for your relationship with God and others.

In the section entitled "Stay in Close Relationship with God" in my *Woman to Woman Mentoring Handbook*, I discuss the importance of God being your primary and priority relationship, from which all other relationships derive.

> The more you focus on your own relationship with God, the better mentor you are going to become. He will guide you and give the direction and answers that you seek. In all our relationships, if we keep our eyes on God instead of the other person, we become more like the Lord. That other person, in this case your mentee, will see that relationship in the way you talk and in your actions.
>
> That is what being a Christian is all about — relationships — and we know it starts with our relationship with Christ. When we are in tune with our Great Mentor, we become more and more like Him. What more could any mentee ask for?

A sure way to put God first in your life is to put Him first in your day: read the Bible, pray, and let God help prioritize your to-do-list. This may require a major realigning of your time, energy, money, and schedule, but the rewards will be tenfold.

PERSONAL PARABLE

Having a quiet time every morning and turning my day over to God helps me prioritize my day's activities and gives me a sense of peace. I know how hard it is when you have a busy family/career life. I just spent three weeks with my daughter, Kim, and her family. Kim has a new baby, and two- and three-year old toddlers. When I first arrived, I started every morning on the run helping with the baby and playing with the kids. But I noticed that I was tired and exhausted all day.

Then I realized the problem. At home, I have a quiet time with the Lord every morning, and at Kim's I was out of my routine. So I reinstated my morning time with the Lord by grabbing a cup of coffee and my Bible and heading out to the back yard or back into my room. When my grandchildren asked what I was doing, my daughter said: "Leave Grammie alone; she's having her quiet time." Soon little Katelyn and Brandon were having their "quiet time" too. Everyone's day went better after that, and what a great witness to my daughter and grandchildren.

Mentoring Moment

Mary first sat at Jesus's feet as a *student*, then as a *servant*. I once heard a pastor say: "Following Jesus cannot be done at a sprint. A fast-paced life and spiritual maturity are incongruous and not compatible." Joanna Weaver points out, "Martha opened her house to Jesus, but that doesn't automatically mean she opened her heart. In her eagerness to serve Jesus, she almost missed the opportunity to *know* Jesus."

Day Two

Assigning Kingdom Value

As my life evolved into a full schedule of writing, speaking, leading the Woman to Woman Mentoring Ministry — while still being a mentor, wife, mother, friend, and Grammie — I had to choose what I could realistically do in 24 hours each day. To help me discern where to put my energy, time, and efforts, I prayerfully came up with the "kingdom value test": Does the task or activity help further God's work on Earth and His eternal kingdom in heaven? If the answer is yes, it has kingdom value. Then the second part of the test is to determine if *I* am the one to do the task or activity.

On Your Own and M&M's

Q: To understand God's view on prioritizing, read Matthew 6:31–34 again today, along with Matthew 4:4 and Luke 12:29–34, and uses these passages to define "kingdom value."

Q: Where do you see Mary applying the kingdom value test?

Q: How can you determine if something has kingdom value in your life?

• How can you use the kingdom value test to establish priorities?

- What can you eliminate that *doesn't* have kingdom value?

- What is something new you feel God is calling you to do that *does* have kingdom value?

Q: Is there a ministry you know God wants you to serve in, but you've been postponing getting involved? Take steps today to join that ministry team and make a difference with your life. Make notes here and brainstorm ministry opportunities.

ON YOUR OWN

Q: If you have been thinking about being a mentor or finding a mentor, please pray about how God might want you to go about that *now*. Don't wait. Valuable time is passing by. You may have to make a choice to give up something in your life, but think of what you will be gaining for the kingdom!

M & M'S

Q: Discuss together if there is something you could do as a team for the kingdom.

Q: Make a list of kingdom value goals you would like to achieve in your time together.

FACE-TO-FACE REFLECTIONS

In Luke 10:42, Jesus gently and tenderly rebuked Martha with a message for us all: the food you are preparing will be eaten and forgotten, but that which Mary is seeking "will not be taken away from her"—what Mary is doing right now has kingdom value. Martha, you must observe Mary. She is role modeling to you what God values most. It is not an either/or choice. We need to eat, but don't make food the priority of this gathering. Don't think eating is more worthy than spending time with Me—the Bread of Life.

Prioritizing my life according to kingdom value means I look at the tasks, activities, and opportunities placed before me every day: then I pray and ask God to help me determine whether or not they have kingdom value, and if He wants me involved. For example, housecleaning certainly keeps God's earthly kingdom presentable. Could someone else do it? Yes. Is it a good use of my time? My answer is, "No." I can be in my office writing a new book or on the road speaking, while a very capable housecleaner cleans my house.

Here is another example. Someone once asked me: "With your frequent traveling schedule, how do you have time to do gardening?" My answer was: "I don't. I have a gardener." Again, I had to ask myself: Does gardening have kingdom value? Flowers certainly are God's creation, but someone else can do the gardening. For me, gardening isn't the best use of my time and energy.

Now don't get me wrong. I am not saying that house cleaning and gardening are not valuable efforts, and for some of you they are enjoyable, fulfilling times to commune with God. I am just saying that with the call on my life to be in full-time ministry and an expanding extended family, I could not do it all. We are not wealthy. We live a modest lifestyle and have a tight budget. I have to give up something else to have these household chores done for me, but that is how I prioritize. Prioritizing usually requires a sacrifice and a choice.

* * *

Mentoring Moment

Never delay doing something for the Lord today because you may not get that opportunity again soon. Prioritizing allows you to choose the "better part." In the *Believer's Bible Commentary* C. A. Coates puts it like this: "The Lord wants to convert us from Marthas into Marys...just as he wants to convert us from lawyers into neighbors."

* * *

Day Three

Balancing Work and Worship

Martha was more concerned about working than worshipping. Martha represents all the people working hard doing good things, but who have no time to worship God. What a paradox. George Campbell Morgan once wisely said: No man can do the work of God until he has the Holy Spirit and is endued with power.

On Your Own and M&M's

Q: Read Acts 13:2–4. How did the Holy Spirit direct Barnabas and Saul (Paul) when they took time to worship *before* going to work?

Q: Who are we working for (Colossians 3:23–24)?

Q: In John 12:8, what was Jesus's message to those who reprimanded Mary for "wasting" oil on His feet?

Q: While Martha focused on the body's hunger and need for food, what did she neglect the soul's hunger and need for (John 6:48)?

Q: Jesus gave a similar message to Martha in Luke 10:41–42. Describe a time when, like Martha, you focused on the work you needed to *do for* Jesus and missed an opportunity to *be with* Him?

- What did you learn from this experience?

Q: Read Matthew 11:28–30. What ideas do these verses give you for how to balance work and worship?

M & M'S

Q: Don't become so focused on achieving your goals such as doing a Bible study or reading a book that you immediately launch into your time together without inviting the Lord to join in and direct your time and maybe even change your focus. Your relationship could become works-oriented rather than worshipful. Has this ever happened to you? Explain.

Q: What are some ways to insure the Lord is the focus of each M&M meeting, and you take time to sit at Jesus's feet together?

FACE-TO-FACE REFLECTIONS

Everything we do requires balance. Good things become harmful when done in excess, with the wrong purpose, or instead of spending time with God. In John 12:8, Jesus did not minimize ministry to the poor. He stressed there will always be poor to minister to, but you won't always have the opportunity to personally commune with Me. And you can't minister effectively until you have spent time with Me.

Jesus sent a similar message to Martha: the frenzied work you are doing to feed us is pointless unless you do it with the right heart that comes from worshipping Me. Where is your peace and joy in serving? Mary honors Me more by listening to me and learning than you do bustling around in a dither upsetting yourself and everyone else.

Martha obviously thought she was *doing* right. From Martha's perspective, maybe it looked like Mary was slacking and relaxing while Martha did all the work. And there is a balance there too. We should never use worship as an excuse to get out of work, or not do our part: this kind of "worship" does not please God. But Martha seemed more concerned about having to work alone than not being with her guests—my sister is not helping me work! Rather than: This is not fair because *I* can't worship You like *she* is. Instead of Martha's work drawing her to Jesus, it distanced her from Him.

Mentoring Moment

The choice isn't between being a *worker* like Martha or a *worshipper* like Mary. What really pleases God is a balance of the two.

"Unless we meet Christ personally and privately every day, we will soon end up like Martha: busy but not blessed. Blessed are the balanced."
—Warren Wiersbe

DAY FOUR

BUSTING BUSYNESS

usyness usually results in ignoring the Lord. Maybe we skip our quiet time or cut our prayertime short. Few things are more damaging to the Christian life than trying to work for Christ without taking time to commune with Christ.

ON YOUR OWN AND M&M'S

Q: How did busyness affect Martha's time with Christ?

Q: How does busyness affect your time with Christ?

● Your relationships?

● Why do you feel a need to be busy?

Q: What does Jesus say in John 15:5 about our efforts to do things on our own?

● What have you been busily trying to do on your own that you need to ask God's assistance?

Q: Pray Psalm 5:3 and Psalm 63:1–8 by personalizing the verses. For example: *In the morning, O LORD, you hear my* [insert your name] *voice; in the morning I* [insert your name] *lay my requests before you and wait in expectation,* Psalm 5:3. Now do the same with Psalm 63:1–8.

● How can you apply the psalmist's description of time with the Lord to your own quiet and devotional time with Him?

● Are you sitting in expectation at Jesus's feet *every* day?

● If not, what can you change to make this the most vital and important time of your day?

Q: How will you "bust busyness" in your life?

M & M'S

Q: Discuss the progress you are making in putting Christ first in your life.

Q: What steps can you take to keep each other accountable and growing in your private personal time with the Lord? Note those ideas here:

Q: Mentor, share any tips you have on busting busyness.

FACE-TO-FACE REFLECTIONS

Mary appears three times in the gospels and, on each occasion, she is in the same place at the feet of Jesus: sitting at His feet listening to Him (Luke 10:39), falling mournfully at His feet as she grieves for Him (John 11:32), and worshipping and pouring out a love offering on His feet (John 12:3). In the *Bible Exposition Commentary*, Warren Wiersbe offers this advice:

> Whenever we criticize others and pity ourselves because we feel overworked, we had better take time to examine our lives. Perhaps in all our busyness, we have been ignoring the Lord. Martha's problem was not that she had too much work to do, but that she allowed her work to distract her and pull her apart. She was trying to serve two masters!...It is vitally important that we spend time at the feet of Jesus every single day, letting Him share His Word with us. *The most important part of the Christian life is the part that only God sees.*

Warren Wiersbe quotes a hymn by Charles Wesley who summarizes it perfectly:

> "Faithful to my Lord's commands,
> I still would choose the better part;
> Serve with careful Martha's hands,
> And loving Mary's heart."

PERSONAL PARABLE

You may have heard the acronym for the word *busy*: B-eing U-nder S-atan's Y-oke. I think that is a very appropriate description. I know in my own life that Satan uses my Type-A personality to keep me feeling like I must have my calendar full and be productive every waking moment. Of course, not only does that cut into my time with the Lord, but it drains me physically and spiritually.

When I started the Woman to Woman Mentoring Ministry, one of my concerns was: Would women take the time to be M&M'S? The mantra I hear from most women these days is, "I'm just so busy." But what a joy it was to watch women discover the value of spending time in a spiritual relationship as they began growing and learning together.

It seems when you are *about His work*, the Lord provides extra energy to accomplish everything *He* thinks is important. My heart breaks when a woman leaves the mentoring ministry because her life is "too busy." It's a sign to me that the world's activities and lures are edging out God, and she's heading for a collision with Satan.

Mentoring Moment

The Lord wants our *salutation* before our *service*.

DAY FIVE

SERVING JOYFULLY AND SELFLESSLY

At the first dinner (Luke 10:38–42), Martha wanted Jesus to know and appreciate how hard she was working for Him. We can only imagine the scowl on her face when she didn't receive the recognition she expected. Sometimes we taint our service with pride and ego. Feeling quite self-righteous, like Martha, our *doing for* Jesus starts to take precedence over *being with* Jesus. A *doing* heart is revealed through our insensitive actions, careless words, and fruitless work.

ON YOUR OWN AND M&M'S

Q: What does 1 Peter 5:5 tell us God feels about pride?

● What does pride lead to—Proverbs 11:2, 18:12?

● What is the antidote to pride?

● How does 1 Peter 5:6–7 provide the recipe for serving selflessly and joyfully?

Q: Proverbs 11:16a (HCSB) says, *"A gracious woman gains honor."* According to Proverbs 18:12, what comes before honor?

Q: When our work doesn't receive the recognition we expect, like Martha, we might vent our displeasure. What does Proverbs 29:11 caution about such a reaction?

Q: How was Mary a role model of gracious humility to Martha's pride and anger?

Q: In 2 Corinthians 9:7, what kind of giving does the Lord say He appreciates?

Q: Characterize your own attitude toward giving your time, energy, and resources in service. Hint: are you busy working *for* the Lord or serving *with* the Lord?

Q: Martha gave warning signals that she had lost perspective of what God values most. What are the warning signals in your own life?

Q: What tool did God give to determine if we are serving with the right attitude and heart (Hebrews 4:12)?

Q: What role model does Philippians 2:4–5 tell us to follow?

M & M'S

Q: How will 2 Corinthians 9:7 and Philippians 2:4–5 influence the time you spend with each other?

FACE-TO-FACE REFLECTIONS

Like Martha, our warning lights of a life full of *doing* instead of *abiding* are things like fatigue, irritability, impatience, edginess, anxiety, and a sense of being out of control. The heart and attitude we serve with determines whether we serve joyfully. Imagine yourself responding to the question "How are you?" with a smile on your face and an enthusiastic "I am just so blessed to be serving the Lord." Or "Praise the Lord; He keeps me so blessedly busy at His work. I feel honored to be used by Him this way." Or "It's such a joy to know that the work I do for Him helps others draw closer to heaven!"

You really can't say these responses with a heavy-burdened heart, can you? Try it—it doesn't work. These words are naturally going to bring a smile on your face, straightening of your stance, and genuine happiness and enthusiasm into your voice. Instead of lamenting, "Oh, I have so very much to do," the Lord fills you anew with His purpose and His plans and you can truly say, "Thank You, Lord, for using me."

Take note, though, that Jesus *gently* rebuked Martha. He didn't minimize her service or attack her character, but instead, expressed genuine concern over her anxiety. His words and attitude conveyed love and compassion. Later, when Martha questioned His handling of her brother's illness, Jesus again was patient and reassured her of His love—and yet, He boldly and patiently confronted her on areas she needed to change in her life. He didn't condone, but He didn't condemn.

Martha didn't argue or become defensive with Jesus. She received His counsel and changed her ways. Jesus's confrontation style is a perfect example for us to follow when we need to confront a fellow believer.

PERSONAL PARABLE

In *He Still Moves Stones*, Max Lucado points out that Martha's attitude was a heart problem:

> The problem is not Mary's choice to listen. The problem is not Martha's choice to host. The problem is Martha's heart, a heart soured with anxiety.... She started bossing God around. Worry will do that to you.... She made a common, yet

dangerous mistake. As she began to work for Him, her work took precedence over her Lord. What began as a way to serve Jesus, slowly and subtly became a way to serve self.... It's easy to forget who is the servant and who is to be served.... With time, our agenda becomes more important than God's. You're more concerned with presenting self than pleasing Him. And you may even find yourself doubting God's judgment. What matters more than the type of service is the heart behind the service. A bad attitude spoils the gift we leave on the altar for God.

Mentoring Moment

A pastor once said, "God is not against service, He just wants us so close to Him that we're not angry about serving."

Gratitude changes your *attitude*!"

FAITH IN ACTION

What one thing from this session does God want you to apply in your life today?

LET'S PRAY

Jesus, please make us willing to sit at Your feet like Mary and learn Your humble ways. Help us to serve You and others with a happy joy-filled heart. Let us remember that the work we do for You is all about You and not about us. Help us to discover what has kingdom value in our life and learn to prioritize by putting You first always. We love You, Lord! Amen.

SESSION FOUR
FACE-TO-FACE WITH MARY AND MARTHA:
SISTERS IN CHRIST

IT'S A MIRACLE!

DAY ONE

A TEST OF FAITH

Most believers still have questions about how God works. We have yet to see *all* the miracles and testimonies Jesus is going to perform in our life. That is why spiritual growth takes time and is a process. Often, we regress as Martha did, and have to refocus and rededicate our life to the pursuit of knowing Christ better each day.

ON YOUR OWN AND M&M'S

Q: Reread the story of the death of Mary's and Martha's brother, Lazarus, in John 11:1–45.

● In verses 21–24, Martha expresses faith, but why isn't it complete faith?

● In verses 25–26, Jesus asks Martha the question presented to someone accepting and professing their faith in Jesus Christ. What was Martha's response in verse 27?

● Do you think this was Martha's first true confession of faith or a rededication of faith?

● Moments later in verse 39, Martha is questioning Jesus again. What does He caution in verse 40 that she must do if she wants to see the glory of God—a miracle?

- Where do you question God, even though you believe?

Q: Can doubt and faith coexist in the same heart at the same time? Why or why not?

Q: What do these verses tell us about faith?
- 2 Corinthians 4:17–18
- Hebrews 11:1
- Hebrews 12:2–4

Q: Read 1 Peter 5:8. Who tries to test our faith?

Q: Read about the armor of God in Ephesians 6:10–18 and then answer these questions:
- Verse 16 tells us to take up the "shield of faith." What does that protect us from?

- What is our weapon for fighting Satan and defending our faith? (Verse 17)

- What are some "flaming arrows" Satan hurls at us to test our faith? (See examples in Psalm 64:2–4 and Jeremiah 9:8)

Q: In Session Two, you contrasted Martha's actions in Luke 10:38–42 with how she prepared the second meal in John 12:1–8. In between those two dinners, Martha had an encounter with Jesus in John 11:1–45. Something dramatic happened to Martha from both her experience on the road with Jesus and the resurrection of her brother Lazarus. How do you think those experiences spiritually matured Martha?

Q: How has an encounter with Jesus grown your faith and the way you worship Jesus now?

Q: Having any doubts about your faith? Seek help from a mentor or pastor who can answer your questions and pray with you.

M&M'S

Q: Mentee, discuss any doubts about your faith, and together pray that God would help you find answers to your questions.

Q: Mentor, if you are unable to answer your mentee's faith questions, go with her to visit a pastor at your church.

FACE-TO-FACE REFLECTIONS

In this study, we have observed Mary exemplifying a godly role model for Martha. We don't really know if Mary was a Christian longer than Martha was, or if Mary simply was the more spiritually mature of the two sisters. When Martha professes that she is a believer (John 11:23), we could speculate that this was the first time she really did acknowledge the deity of Jesus. This could be the point where her eyes opened, and she finally did *get it*: the belief that Jesus was the Messiah moved from head knowledge to her heart. Or perhaps her words were a rededication or confirmation of her faith.

Sometimes believers critically surmise that people who still have spiritual questions are not Christians. That may or may not be true, but we need to be sensitive to the spiritual growth stage of others. It is prideful for those of us who are spiritually older to see ourselves as superior to those who are still learning. And if we were honest, we would have to admit that at times we too have questions about God because we won't ever understand everything this side of heaven.

As so often happens when I am writing, my devotional this morning was on the topic I was writing about, doubt and faith:

Many of our "what ifs" are strategically suggested by the enemy of God; many of them are the natural thinking of a fallen flesh. Either way, we are restless within until we are able to rest in God.... That's part of the reason for prayer—extended, persistent, worshipful prayer. It brings us from a place of doubt to a place of faith. Once we're there, God can answer according to His Word.... Our worship reminds us of who He is. And knowing who He is will nurture faith like nothing else.... Wisdom begins with a knowledge of who God is and wisdom is often a prerequisite to faith. We cannot approach God in belief unless we have first determined that His will toward us is good.

—Chris Tiegreen, *The One Year Walk with God Devotional*, July 23 devotional

PERSONAL PARABLE

The armor of God in Ephesians 6:10–18 is a prayer that we can personalize and pray to protect ourselves from Satan. My husband and I pray these verses every morning and wouldn't consider going about our day without prayerfully putting on: the belt of truth, the breastplate of righteousness, the shoes of the gospel of peace, the shield of faith, the helmet of salvation, and the sword of the Spirit, which is the Word of God. I would like to challenge you also to prayerfully fit yourself for spiritual battle daily and see how much better your day goes.

Mentoring Moment

"Faith sees the invisible,
believes the unbelievable,
and receives the impossible."
—Corrie Ten Boom

DAY TWO

WAITING TOGETHER

We've all heard this advice: You just need to wait on the Lord. But waiting can be a very lonely time. In John 11:3, the sisters sent word to Jesus: "Lord, the one you love is sick." Then they waited.

ON YOUR OWN AND M&M'S

Q: Read John 11:3–7. What do you think was going through Mary's and Martha's minds when Jesus did not come immediately?

● What would have gone through your mind?

Q: Read John 11:20. How did each sister respond to Jesus's delayed arrival?

● How did their responses fit their individual personalities and temperaments?

● How do you react when you don't get a quick answer to your prayers or God doesn't answer the way you think He should?

Q: Based on your reading of Jesus's response to Lazarus's death in John 11:33–35,38, how do you think Jesus feels about our pain when He chooses for us to wait on Him to reveal a divine plan that is much bigger than merely the relief from our present suffering?

Q: How do Psalm 33:20–22 and Psalm 130:5,7 provide comfort while we wait?

M & M'S

Q: Some of you may not have seen the progress you hoped for in your M&M relationship, or you have unfulfilled expectations. What has been your reaction to your disappointment?

● How do you see through the story of Mary, Martha, and Lazarus that Jesus may have a reason for the delay?

● How would you react if you knew Jesus had a miracle waiting for you?

FACE-TO-FACE REFLECTIONS

Do not let the currents of your circumstances dictate the direction you'll take. That's God's domain.... We must learn to see Him as the unconstrained God, the God who is not limited by the gaping need of our situation or the restrictiveness of our circumstances. Why does God work this way? Maybe simply because it brings Him greater glory. When we take only humanly possible steps, we give our humanity the credit. God alone deserves the praise for overcoming impossibilities. Miracles point to Him. Expect them. Ask for them.
— Chris Tiegreen, *The One Year Walk with God Devotional,*
July 24 devotional

On November 16, 1993, I started daily journaling and praying for a miracle—my daughter Kim's salvation. Then I waited and prayed, even as she moved farther away from the Lord. At one point, when I was desperately crying out to God, the Lord assured me He wanted her salvation more than I did. That was a comforting reminder that only He could soften my daughter's heart, and so I persistently and hopefully prayed daily—and waited.

Five years later, on November 1, 1998, my husband and I had the joy of baptizing Kim and Toby, her fiancé, and they were married in a Christian wedding on November 14, 1998. I look at them sitting next to us in church, and I am so glad I didn't give up on God. I was just praying for their salvation, but the Lord gave us an experience together in their baptism that was beyond my wildest expectations and prayers. The wait was well worth the miracle. If you'd like to read their story in more detail, may I suggest *Praying for Your Prodigal Daughter*.

* * *

Mentoring Moment

God is sometimes early, but He is never late. Or, as some put it, "He may not come when you want Him, but He is always on time."

* * *

DAY THREE

CRISIS MENTORING

eing a mentor really is easy: It's simply being you and letting someone else watch how you do life as a follower of Jesus Christ — even in a crisis.

ON YOUR OWN AND M&M'S

Q: Mary was not only a spiritual role model for Martha, but others in the community were also watching and following her — John 11:19, 28–31. How did Mary's doubtful lament to Jesus in John 11:32 create doubt in those who observed her (John 11:37)?

● How was Mary and the mourners' faith restored in John 11:45?

Q: Contrast Paul's admission of his struggle with sin in Romans 7:21–25 with his willingness to be a role model for others to follow in 1 Corinthians 11:1.

Q: How do Mary's moment of doubt and Paul's struggle with sin give you confidence that you don't have to be perfect in order to be a role model?

Mary's acts of love and worship were public, spontaneous, sacrificial, lavish, personal, affectionate—no concern for ridicule or embarrassment. Mary was loyal to Jesus while He was still alive. Others didn't understand His deity until after His death. Mary fully understood who Jesus was and worshipped Him as sovereign while He was among them. Yet, Mary was not perfect. No human can reach a perfection of faith here on earth. We all still struggle with doubts when our faith is tested. But Jesus is the "Perfect Role Model." Praying and reading about the examples Jesus left for us in the Bible will restore our faith—and that is exactly the perfect role model for those who are watching us.

PERSONAL PARABLE

In Session Two, I mentioned rededicating my life at a Harvest Crusade, led by Pastor Greg Laurie. Just last week, Pastor Greg's firstborn, 33-year-old son died in a tragic car accident. Because Pastor Greg is a well-known evangelist, both in our area and around the world, newspapers covered the tragic story. The world was watching.

Three days after the accident, Pastor Greg spoke to his congregation on Sunday morning. The short talk appeared on YouTube, and the local newspaper ran a full-page article. Here are several excerpts from Pastor Greg's eulogy of his son: "My son wasn't perfect. My son was a prodigal at times, but he came back. He really committed his life to Christ in the last two years of his life. He couldn't have been in a better place spiritually. I still believe," he said with a smile. "The Lord is with me, our faith is true, and in the darkest hour, He will be with you too. You don't have to be afraid." The heading on the YouTube video was "I Still Believe."

I also watched the memorial service on my computer and both of the pastors who spoke used the passage we have been studying, John 11:1–45.

Mentoring Moment

Mary, Martha, and Pastor Greg Laurie mourned and grieved their losses, as well they should, but Pastor Greg knows what Mary and Martha were soon to find out—the grave has no hold over believers.

DAY FOUR

GOD ALWAYS HAS A PLAN

oth Mary and Martha believed that Jesus could heal their sick brother Lazarus (John 11:21,32). However, they had an expectation of how and when it should happen. They thought Jesus would come promptly—certainly *before* Lazarus died. That is a natural assumption, isn't it?

ON YOUR OWN AND M&M'S

Q: How did Jesus feel about Mary, Martha, and Lazarus (John 11:3, 5)?

Q: Jesus loved Mary and Martha, but He still didn't do what they wanted. Describe a time in your life when Jesus answered your prayers in a completely different way than you asked.
● What was the outcome?

● Was it beyond what you could have ever thought to ask?

Q: In John 11:39, Jesus was about to raise Lazarus from the dead: an incredible plan! However, just when Jesus said, "Take away the stone" from in front of Lazarus's tomb, what was Martha's response?

- How was her response typical of what you have observed about Martha's temperament and personality?

Q: Has God ever wanted to miraculously resurrect something in your life—maybe a marriage you thought was over, a child who seemed hopelessly lost, a relationship that ended badly—and you told Jesus He didn't understand that the situation was too smelly, painful, and hard? Describe that situation.

Q: What situation currently in your life needs a resurrection—a miracle?

- If you are doubtful that God could resurrect the situation, pray Job 42:2 for confidence and renewed faith.

Q: How can you find comfort from Proverbs 19:21 and Jeremiah 29:11 when things aren't going as *you* planned?

Q: How can we align our plans with God's (Proverbs 16:3)?

M & M'S

Q: How have you seen God's plan in matching you together as M&M'S?

Q: Do you have any ideas about the plans He has for your relationship?

FACE-TO-FACE REFLECTIONS

Martha blatantly told Jesus He didn't know what He was doing! When crisis happens in our life, it's natural to ask God, "If you love me, why did You let this happen?" Our first thought seldom is: *I wonder what miracle God has planned?* But Jeremiah 29:11 does assure us that in a believer's life God will work *all* things out for His good—which will ultimately be for our good. It's just that sometimes God's and our definition of good is different. But in his August 5 devotional, Chris Tiegreen reminds us, "Biblical prayers must eventually fall in line with the biblical agenda: displaying the glory of God. There is no better way to gain victory in crisis than to shift our focus from our purposes to God's."

Mary and Martha could not readily see God's plan as they mourned the death of their brother and wondered at the absence of their dear friend, Jesus. Little did they know that Jesus had a bigger plan in mind than merely healing Lazarus: a plan that would offer eternal life.

PERSONAL PARABLE

We once had a woman in the mentoring ministry give a testimony that her marriage was dead. She and her husband were separated and filing for divorce—the love was gone. In the process of burying their marriage, her health began to fail and they were both suffering greatly. At that time, the couple were non-practicing Mormons, but a doctor told them about Jesus, and they became Christians and Jesus restored their marriage. I will never forget her words as she shared her story and ended with "Our God is truly a God of resurrections. He took a marriage that was completely dead and brought it back to life better than it ever was before."

•   •   •

Mentoring Moment

People see God's plans and purpose at work
when situations are out of their control
and look impossible.

"Miracles always magnify God."
— Pastor Tim Westcott

•   •   •

DAY FIVE

GOD STILL WORKS MIRACLES!

*M*iracles still do happen!" I exclaim at every Woman to Woman Mentoring Celebration Potluck at the end of the M&M six-month commitment. Incredible miracles occur when two women walk side-by-side with Christ at the center of their relationship. We have literally seen marriages saved, wayward children return to the family, parents and husbands accept Christ, even mentees accepting the Lord through the loving and prayerful example of their mentor.

ON YOUR OWN AND M&M'S

Q: Write your own definition of the word *miracle*.

Q: Now look up *miracle* in the dictionary. How does your definition compare?

Q: Read how Jesus miraculously fed more than 5,000 (John 6:1–15).
● What did Jesus ask Philip (v. 5)?

● Why did Jesus ask Philip that question (v. 6)?

● What was Philip's response (v. 7)?

- How did the people who observed the feeding react (v. 14)?

Q: Read how Jesus healed the man born blind (John 9:1–41).
- What was the the blind man's neighbors' reaction (8–12)?

- What impact did the miracle have on the blind man? (35–38)

Q: How did Jesus's resurrection of the widow's son in Luke 7:11–17 and Peter's resurrection of Dorcas in Acts 9:40–42 impact the believers and unbelievers who witnessed the miracle?

Q: Explain why Jesus waited until Lazarus was dead four days before He came (John 11:4–5,14, 41).

Q: How did Jesus's resurrection of Lazarus impact unbelievers and doubters who witnessed the miracle (John 11:37,45; 12:9–11)?

- What impact did it have on the believers (John 11:40)?

- Why didn't everyone become believers (John 11:46–48)?

Q: What impact do miracles have on you?

Q: What is the common purpose—past and present—of all miracles? (Hint: Psalm 72:18–19; Luke 7:16; John 6:14; 9:3–5, 39; 11:4, 45; Acts 9:42;)

Q: When God performed a spiritual "resurrection" in your life, were others watching? Explain:

Q: William MacDonald wrote in *The Believer's Bible Commentary* in reference to the resurrection of Lazarus that "Only Christ can raise the dead, but He gives us the task of removing stones of stumbling, and of unwinding the graveclothes of prejudice and superstition."

● What does this quote mean to you?

Q: Who needs you to help remove stumbling stones and unwind graveclothes of prejudice and superstition in her life?

● How and when will you offer that help?

M & M'S

Q: Are there still any stones of stumbling or graveclothes of prejudice and superstition in your lives? If so, what are they?

Q: How might you help each other overcome these obstacles?

FACE-TO-FACE REFLECTIONS

Dorothy Kelley Paterson and Rhonda H. Kelley discuss miracles' impact in the *Women's Evangelical Commentary New Testament:*

Jesus was never guilty of "bad timing." He knew that the glory of God would be displayed in this tragedy. The resurrection of Lazarus would strengthen faith in the followers of Christ, while moving unbelievers toward Him. Their pain would not be in vain. As disciples, Mary and Martha held tenaciously to their faith, and in God's timing, the truth was revealed to them. They saw the glory of God and even came to understand His ultimate purpose for their trial. They witnessed an incredible miracle that confirmed a universal truth: God has the power to raise the dead. He can transform a hopeless predicament into a glorious victory. Tragedy was an opportunity for God to manifest His sovereignty, power, and love.... Sometimes God allows genuine needs to go unmet temporarily, which could result in deep pain. However, He can then bring about a greater good through the experience of suffering for His glory and for the strengthening of faith.

Jesus wanted to perform a miracle in front of His disciples, Mary, Martha, the mourners and bystanders (John 11:19) so the doubters would be convinced that He truly was the Messiah, the Savior, the Son of God. And that is the purpose of *all* miracles — glorification of God and salvation of people. If you are a believer, you have experienced the greatest miracle of all: you were dead in transgression and sin and made alive again in Christ!

PERSONAL PARABLE

I know firsthand about God's miraculous plans that display His glory. My daughter, Kim, and her husband, Toby, struggled with infertility. After many tears and "why prayers," they finally accepted that God had a different plan — adoption. Within a year of aligning their plans with God's plan, they adopted my precious Hispanic grandson, Brandon. Little did we all know that when they received Brandon, Kim was already pregnant with my sweet granddaughter Katelyn! And two years later, Kim just gave birth to precious Sienna. Kim and Toby see clearly now what they couldn't see through the heartbreak of infertility——that God's plan was for Brandon to have a loving home and then He resurrected Kim's barren womb.

Kim and Toby had the opportunity publicly to give God the glory when their pastor asked if they would give their testimony of the miracle of adopting baby Brandon and then discovering they were pregnant with miracle baby Katelyn. The pastor's sermon that morning was "God's Still in the Miracle Business!" I quoted the words of my prayer journal that December 3, 2006, 18 months before Sienna was born, in my book *Praying for Your Prodigal Daughter*:

"Today I observed a miracle! ... I was the proud parent and Grammie snapping pictures and listening to Kim give God all the glory and praise for her two children. She talked about her own plan for how she and Toby would start a family, but it didn't happen that way.... Then Toby told of the numerous people praying for them to become parents. There stood my daughter and her husband with microphones in their hands, exclaiming the power of prayer. The same daughter who had been so embarrassed by her mother's prayers was now giving a public testimony of answered prayers in her life! Isn't that just like You, God, to bring it full circle."

Mentoring Moment

Jesus's raising of Lazarus from the dead was the next to last miracle He did while on earth, and yet, because Jesus lives in our heart, He is still performing miracles in our lives today.

FAITH IN ACTION

What one thing from this session does God want you to apply in your life today?

LET'S PRAY TOGETHER

Lord, thank You for still performing miracles. Help us to be patient and not waiver in our faith when things don't turn out the way we think they should. Remind us to pray the armor of God, to remember that faith is believing in things we cannot see, and to remember that You see everything. Amen.

SACRIFICE UNTO THE LORD

Day One

Miracles May Require Sacrifice

On August 5, 2001, the Taliban arrested eight Christian aides working for Shelter Now International on charges of spreading Christianity, a crime punishable by death in Afghanistan. Two of these missionaries were American women, Heather Mercer, only 18 years old, and Dayna Curry. I first read of the arrests in a small article buried in the back of the newspaper. The Lord put on my heart to pray for these two women and daily scan the paper for more news about their fate, but the articles were infrequent.

All that changed with the attack on the World Trade Center on September 11, 2001, and the ensuing hunt in Afghanistan for Osama bin Laden and the Taliban suspected of initiating the terrorist attacks. Overnight, the world became aware that Christians were on trial by the Taliban for proselytizing. Suddenly, newspaper articles about the missionaries appeared in prominent places, often on the front page. Nightly, parents of the imprisoned Christians pleaded in televised interviews for the release of their children. Relatives appeared on TV talk shows, and magazines covered the vigil of friends, family, and churches praying around the clock for the two American girls' release. The news media followed their story as the situation became more precarious when the United States attacked Afghanistan and Kabul, the very city of the missionaries' imprisonment.

Media coverage often mentioned the numerous Americans praying for the two girls and it featured their home church in Waco, Texas, holding 24-hour prayer vigils for the women. The parents were understandably anxious about the fate of their children, but publicly they expressed faith and hope. As reports came of the girls starting to wear down under the stress, Heather's father offered to trade places with his daughter, but the Taliban refused.

As the war in Afghanistan raged on, the prisoners heard the U.S. and its allies bombing all around them as they tried to capture and disband the Taliban. At one point, the Taliban offered to negotiate the release of the missionaries if America would call off the attacks. The American government refused, knowing that while many innocent lives were lost on September 11, even more surely would follow if the Taliban terrorists force remained intact.

On Wednesday, November 14, 2001, "It was like a miracle," said George Taubmann, one of the eight prisoners and head of Shelter Now in Afghanistan. The retreating Taliban had fled from Kabul, taking the prisoners with them to a prison in Ghazni, 50 miles from the capital. As this area came under heavy bombardment, Northern Alliance fighters burst into the prison and were shocked to see the missionaries imprisoned there. Rejoicing in their find, they set the prisoners free. It truly was a miracle!

Front page headlines proclaimed the news: "Aide Worker's Family Had Faith She Would Be Freed!" "Churches Celebrate Detainees' Release." The media carried to a waiting and interested world the news of the Christians' release as an answer to prayers: To God be the glory!

ON YOUR OWN AND M&M'S

Q: Explain the similarities between God waiting to answer the prayers for the release of the Christian missionaries imprisoned in Afghanistan and the story of Jesus waiting to answer Mary's and Martha's prayers for Lazarus (John 11:6). As you think about the parallels between the modern-day and biblical stories, use the following questions as a guide and take a spiritual perspective (not military or political) on the parallels:

- Why do you think the missionaries had to stay in prison for so long? (Why did Lazarus have to die and be in the tomb for four days? See John 11:38–39.)

- Why during wartime? (Who was warring against Jesus when Lazarus died? See John 11:8, 46–47.)

- Why didn't God just release the missionaries through negotiations with the United States? (Why didn't Jesus supernaturally heal Lazarus?)

- Why wasn't a father allowed to take the place of his daughter? (What was Lazarus's death and resurrection foreshadowing? What Father could not take the place of His Son? See John 11:51–52.)

- How was God glorified in the missionaries' release? (In Lazarus's resurrection? See John 11:4.)

Q: How does John 11:4 provide one answer as to why God lets sickness happen?

Q: Have you seen Jesus ask you to sacrifice while He delayed answers to your prayers so that He could perform a miracle to show His glory? Describe the circumstances:

- Were others watching, waiting, and sacrificing with you?

- This is a testimony that needs telling. Read Psalm 66:16–20 for a format of how to write out your testimony. Make notes:

Q: Who can you share your testimony with today? Who needs to be comforted by knowing that Jesus is alive and among us and that He still cares about them?

M&M'S

Q: Use the answered prayers you have seen in your M&M relationship to write together an account of when and how God answered them. This is your mentoring testimony. Be sure to note if you saw "miracles."

Q: See if you can share your mentoring testimony together at your church. Many would be blessed.

FACE-TO-FACE REFLECTIONS

Whenever anyone tells me about a difficult or amazing incident in his or her life, I always advise journaling to help remember all God is doing in the midst of the circumstance. This is a person's testimony of God's faithfulness in a believer's life. These life circumstances are not solely for our own character building, but also for us to lead others to our Lord and Savior, Jesus Christ. We must share our story—willingly, openly, vulnerably, and sacrificially. Our story becomes our *testimony* when we give God the glory for the miracle. It gives purpose to whatever sacrifice we've had to make.

The sick man at Bethesda *"went and told the Jews that it was Jesus who had made him well"* (John 5:15). The blind man testified to his fellow Jews, *"'I was blind but now I see!'* . . . *Nobody has ever heard of opening the eyes of a man born blind. If this man [Jesus] were not from God, he could do nothing'"* (John 9:25, 32–33). Eighteen-year-old Heather Mercer, her friend and fellow missionary Dayna Curry, and I, as well as many other men and women, have written books to testify to the world that God still performs miracles today. What will you do to share the miracles God has done in your life?

PERSONAL PARABLE

My breast cancer diagnosis was shocking. We prayed for a cure, but like Lazarus, Jesus didn't cure me—that time. Instead, He revealed a purpose that was bigger than my pain and sadness. After I completed the initial cancer surgery and treatment, I began to see God's larger plan, which transformed my suffering into a tool for His glory. Now I could speak and write with more compassion to those women who were going through a tragic time in their life. I also knew He wanted me to mentor other breast-cancer sisters by writing the book I longed for during my breast cancer journey. I couldn't have written *Dear God, They Say It's Cancer: A Companion Guide for Women on the Breast Cancer Journey* had I not had breast cancer myself. Writing that book was a sacrifice of love because it was a time of life I would have rather forgotten. But just today, I was able to give my book to a young mother in our church who will be having breast cancer surgery in a few weeks. Every time I hear from a woman comforted by my book, I know my sacrifice is bringing God glory.

Several years after my surgery, it seemed the cancer had returned, requiring another surgery. But when I arrived for the pre-op, they couldn't find the area of concern. It was gone. Later that morning as I sat having breakfast with my husband and my friend and her husband, who were going to sit with my husband during my surgery, my friend's husband said, "I have never seen a miracle before!"

Recent tests have revealed a recurrence of the cancer — not life threatening — but requiring additional surgery. Now I can relate to the many women in my book who wrote of recurrences and the additional ones God will put in my path as I claim John 11:4 (HCSB), *"This sickness will not end in death but is for the glory of God, so that the Son of God may be glorified through it."*

To God be the glory, again!

Mentoring Moment

God tries our faith so that we may try His faithfulness.

DAY TWO

THE ULTIMATE SACRIFICE

When Mary selflessly and humbly anointed Jesus's head and feet with perfume, she received a blessing. Jesus said people always would remember what she did, and we do. Three gospels mention her anointing Jesus.

ON YOUR OWN AND M&M'S

Q: Read the account of Mary's sacrificial anointing of Jesus in Matthew 26:6–13, Mark 14:3–9, and John 12:1–8.

Q: Read Hebrews 9:24–28. For what ultimate sacrifice was Mary preparing Jesus?

Q: How do Romans 12:1 and Ephesians 5:1 tell us to imitate Christ's sacrifice?

Q: How are you making a "living sacrifice" unto the Lord in the following areas:
- Your time?

- Your money?

- Your ministry?

- Your energy?

- Your relationships?

- Your relationship to Christ?

- For others?

Q: Read Matthew 26:38–39, 42. How do these verses change your perspective on your sacrifice of service for the Lord?

Q: What ultimate sacrifice does Jesus ask of us?
- Psalm 51:16–17
- John 15:12–13,17
- Hebrews 13:14–16

Q: What does the Lord want from us even more than our sacrifice? (See Proverbs 21:3.)

Q: Pray that the Lord frees you of any hold that money and possessions have on you. Ask God to give you a heart that wants to give all it has to Him. Do you need to do a study on sacrificial serving, giving, tithing, or maybe look up some Scriptures on what Jesus thinks of a cheerful giver? If so, make a promise to yourself here to do just that.

M & M'S

Q: What sacrifices have you made to maintain your M&M relationship?

Q: How have you seen God bless the time and effort you both made to this commitment?

Q: How might others talk about your M&M relationship for years to come (Matthew 26:12)?

FACE-TO-FACE REFLECTIONS

The *American College Dictionary* defines *sacrifice* as "the offering of life (animal, plant, or human or some material possession etc.), to a deity, as in propitiation or homage. The surrender or destruction of something prized or desirable for the sake of something considered as having a higher or more pressing claim."

Mary's oil was a love offering: much beyond a tithe. Spices and ointments were costly in those days and had to be imported. The oil was negotiable on the open market and often used as an investment. It may have represented Mary's life savings. But nothing was too good for the Savior who had returned her brother to life and would soon give His own life for her.

Sitting at Jesus's feet among the male guests listening and learning had to cause quite a stir, and yet, Mary didn't let it intimidate her. She went against the tradition of the day and sacrificed her reputation to become a disciple of Jesus. There was much prejudice against women in their culture, but Jesus showed women respect, and like Mary, many followed Him (Mark 15:40–42).

If Martha was part owner of the oil, she gave her blessing on Mary pouring it over Jesus. The Scriptures don't mention Martha as one of the protestors. Martha assumed the more traditional female role of preparing food, but she also risked her reputation, and maybe her life, by being friends with the controversial Jesus.

We "tsk–tsk" Martha's audacity to tell Jesus that she was overworked and overwhelmed in serving Him, yet, how often do we ourselves do the same thing? The next time these thoughts come to your mind about your ministry and service for the Lord, visualize yourself saying those words into Jesus's loving eyes and looking at His nail scarred hands and feet. He wasn't too busy or overworked to make the sacrifice to serve us with His life. Can we do any less for Him?

Mentoring Moment

Sacrifice what is *easy* for what is *best*.
If it's easy, it probably isn't significant.

DAY THREE

THE FRAGRANCE OF SACRIFICE

*S*criptures refer to the fragrance that permeated the house when Mary anointed Jesus with her fragrant offering of worship. Martha was the source of the food aroma as she worked away in the kitchen and the fragrance filled the house of baking bread, olive oil, roasted vegetables, maybe even frying fish, or roasting lamb. Sometimes, we overlook the fact that Martha represents the fragrance that can come from the work we do for the Lord when we do it unto His glory and not our own.

ON YOUR OWN AND M&M'S:

Q: Each time Mary sat at Jesus's feet, Scripture records a fragrance.
● What is the fragrance in Luke 10?

● In John 11?

● What are the two fragrances in John 12?

Q: Describe the aroma of sacrifice and offering in each of these Old Testament passages:
● Genesis 8:20–21
● Exodus 29:18,25,41

Q: How does Paul describe sacrifice in each of these New Testament passages?
● Ephesians 5:1–2

● Philippians 4:18

Q: How does 2 Corinthians 2:14–16 describe sharing Christ with others?

Q: How is your life a pleasing aroma to the Lord?

● Has it ever been a stench to the Lord? Explain:

M & M'S

Q: How will the legacy of your M&M relationship be a sweet aroma to the Lord?

FACE-TO-FACE REFLECTIONS

The *NIV Study Bible* notes for 2 Corinthians 2:16 explain: "As the gospel aroma is released in the world through Christian testimony, it is always sweet-smelling, even though it may be differently received."

Today our churches fill with the fragrance of Jesus as we worship Him. Pray that His fragrance stays with you even after you leave the church. Our goal as Christians should be to continuously offer our life and testimony as a pleasing aroma — a fragrant offering — onto the Lord. Brother Andrew once said, "Real holiness has a fragrance about it which is its own."

When I stay at my daughter's house, I awaken every morning to a wonderful coffee aroma drifting into my room. My son-in-law, Toby, arises early every morning and makes the coffee for us, and as I lie in bed enjoying my favorite morning fragrance, I think of the sacrifice Toby makes every day to work hard to support his family.

Mentoring Moment

The *Believer's Bible Commentary* quotes Charles R. Erdman, "While the Master does appreciate all that we undertake for Him, He knows that our first need is to sit at His feet and learn His will; then in our tasks we shall be calm and peaceful and kindly, and at last our service may attain the perfectness of that of Mary when in a later scene she poured upon the feet of Jesus the ointment, the perfume of which still fills the world."

Day Four

Risky Sacrifice

*S*acrifice by its very definition means giving up something we value, which just could be our security and safety.

ON YOUR OWN AND M&M'S

Q: What did Mary risk in anointing Jesus (Matthew 26:8–9, John 12:3–7)?

Q: What did Mary, Martha, and Lazarus risk by being friends of Jesus (John 11:46–53)?

Q: What did Jesus risk in publicly performing the miracle of Lazarus's resurrection (John 11:8, 46–57)?

Q: What did Lazarus risk by Jesus raising him from the dead (John 12:9–11)?

Q: How did Jesus feel about Mary, Martha, and Lazarus (John 11:3, 5, 11)?

Q: Describe a time when you took a risk by being a friend of Jesus:

M & M'S

Q: Have you had to risk anything for being M&M'S?

Q: Talk together about how to respond to any friends or relatives who might challenge your relationship. Make some notes:

FACE-TO-FACE REFLECTIONS

Sometimes being a mentor is tough duty and risky. Mentoring does take time, there is no tangible pay, and it may mean having to deal with uncomfortable areas in the other woman's life, just as Jesus had to do with Martha. Being a mentor may mean misunderstanding and ridicule by others who think you are wasting your time, just as Mary received for *"wasting the precious perfume."* When we choose to serve God publicly, we open ourselves to criticism. Some may try to persuade you that you don't have time to mentor and there are better things to do with your time and energy. Others may say you don't know enough to mentor or aren't worthy. Some advise, "be firmer," some say "be more lenient," still others question the advice you give. Your children or friends might feel replaced by your mentee. They may experience feelings of jealousy and resent the time you spend with her.

As a mentee, your mom, husband/boyfriend, or friends might wonder why you go to someone else besides them for wise counsel. Their feelings might get hurt, and they may try to interfere with meetings with your mentor or ridicule and discount her advice.

Hopefully, none of these scenarios happens to you, but if they do, turn them into an opportunity to give a testimony and witness about the blessings of mentoring.

When I first quit my career to go into full-time lay ministry, my husband lost his job three months later. Even our Christian friends and family could not understand how I continued in unpaid ministry during this time. When I shared with my daughter, Kim, about the Woman to Woman Mentoring Ministry, she always asked, "Mom, are you getting paid for that?" She didn't have a relationship with Jesus yet, but still I tried to explain that my payment was in changed lives and the blessings I saw as women experienced the wonder of an M&M relationship. I would tell her, "You can't put a dollar figure on that!" I knew by her exasperated shrug of her shoulders and rolling of her eyes that she didn't understand what I was saying. I prayed that someday she would...and today she does!

The name of my writing and speaking ministry, About His Work Ministries, evolved from the answer my husband and I gave to people during this "unemployment" season. When people asked if I was going back to work, my husband would answer, "She is working. She is about the Lord's work." We have made many "risky" sacrifices for the ministry, and we would do it all again to hear the Lord say when we meet Him Face-to-Face, "Well done, my good and faithful servants."

Mentoring Moment

As Christians, we understand sacrifice —
it is the basis of our faith.

DAY FIVE

TEAMWORK IS SACRIFICE

My daughter, Kim, is now a Christian, and she *gets* sacrifice! She watches and observes the Lord bless the fragrant offering of all that my husband and I have given to Him. Like my daughter, Martha must have been taking it all in. By the time of the anointing of Jesus, Martha was no longer questioning her sister's actions. In fact, we read of her quietly preparing a meal in the kitchen and serving everyone while Mary anointed Jesus in the living room. Finally, they learned how to serve together and how to combine their gifts, talents, and styles of worship into a team.

ON YOUR OWN AND M&M'S

Q: Even when animosity exists, family usually unifies in a crisis or tragedy. How did Mary and Martha work together when faced with their brother's illness? (See John 11:3, 28–29.)

Q: How did they work together as a team at the dinner in John 12:1–3?

Q: How did Jesus's disciples work together as a team to support Jesus in going to Lazarus? (See John 11:16.)

Q: Are you participating on a team for Christ's work? If your answer is no, perhaps God is calling you to offer your spiritual gifts and talents to serve with others. If yes, what have you learned from the study of Mary and Martha that will help you to be a better team member?

ON YOUR OWN

Consider that God might be calling you to become part of an M&M team as a mentor or mentee. The sacrifice of time and energy will be a sweet sacrifice unto the Lord and you will receive a tenfold blessing.

M & M'S

Q: Have you seen yourselves become a team? If yes, describe.

- If no, how could you add teamwork to your relationship? For example: working in a ministry or starting a ministry together, or going on a mission trip together. Think big!

Q: How will you use your relationship as a testimony of the Lord's greatness?

Q: If you haven't seen it yet, God has a plan. We have many testimonies of women wondering what God, (and we) were thinking when we matched them as M&M'S, and then they had a glorious, miraculous testimony in the end.

Q: Don't let this study be the end of your time together. There are other studies in the "Face-to-Face" series that you might enjoy doing together.

At the second supper, Mary and Martha seemed to have worked out the distribution of duties. Maybe Mary pitched in and helped Martha in the kitchen before Jesus and the guests arrived, and while she peeled and chopped the veggies she confided in Martha what she planned to do with the oil. Knowing in advance about the sacred moment to come, Martha knew her sister was working, too—doing the Lord's work.

There have been many M&M'S who have teamed up to start spin-off ministries from the Woman to Woman Mentoring Ministry. In one M&M relationship, both women were wives of unbelieving husbands and they started a ministry together called "Charmed Influence." Other M&M'S create gift baskets for Easter and Mother's Day to take to homes for abused women and children.

PERSONAL PARABLE

On the DVD that accompanies the *Woman to Woman Mentoring DVD Leader Kit* and in the accompanying *Coordinator's Guide*, there is a three-generational M&M testimony. All three women, Marcy, Donna, and Lisa, were perfect strangers when they first met, and yet the Lord truly did the matching as you see astonishing common threads weave through all their lives. On the DVD, you hear these three women share the incredible way they saw God at work in their M&M relationships.

Marcy came to the ministry as a new Christian with a struggling marriage. She participated as a mentee in an M&M relationship, and then went on to be a mentor seven times—a sacrifice of both love and time. Her first mentee was Donna, and they later discovered that Marcy had the same birthday as Donna's recently deceased mother: what an affirmation that was to the two of them that God was instrumental in their being matched as M&M'S! After having Marcy mentor her, Donna felt led to be a mentor to mentee Lisa.

Lisa shares her initial disappointment with Donna, a woman her own age, when she wanted a mother figure. But Lisa says that her faith and prayers kept her in the relationship, as she sacrificed her idea of a perfect mentor. Now Lisa is so glad she didn't give up because God knew that Donna was just the friend she needed, and they have stayed lifelong friends.

These three M&M'S teamed together to share their testimony for new M&M'S at Saddleback's Woman to Woman Mentoring Ministry and then participated in the making of the DVD for the *Woman to Woman Mentoring DVD Leader Kit*. And I show that DVD *every* time I speak on mentoring. The legacy of their three-generation testimony reaches around the world.

* * *

Mentoring Moment

Sacrificial obedience is the ultimate act of worship.

* * *

FAITH IN ACTION

What one thing from this session does God want you to apply in your life today?

LET'S PRAY TOGETHER

Lord, it's so easy to become caught up in the things we want and forget about the things You want us to give up and sacrifice for You. Help us be aware of how You want to use us both individually and as M&M'S. We want to make a difference in the world for You, and we want our life to be a sweet fragrance that pleases You. Amen.

Face-to-Face with Mary and Martha

A Sisters in Christ Testimony

Rosalie Campbell

I entered a mentoring relationship through the back door in 1983. It was a bittersweet time for me. I mourned my father's death, yet celebrated because I had repented from a wayward lifestyle; and accepted Christ in my life. The pastor of the church that I attended recommended I meet with a lady named Doris, who would have more time to work with me; he sensed we would be compatible. How right he was. Doris had a heart calling from God to guide me as a new believer. I didn't seek a mentor, but God arranged a divine appointment for me through one of His servants.

Doris did more than guide me; she became my friend, encourager, discipler, and mentor. The mentoring relationship between Doris and I resembled that of two close sisters. Although she was six years older than I was, we discovered we had many mutual interests and character traits. After the initial getting acquainted time, we decided to do a weekly Bible study together. She taught me many truths of the Bible and showed me ways to apply those principles to my life. Her love of God was infectious.

Once bonded, we laughed and cried together, shared our struggles and successes, confided our hopes and dreams. For two years, Doris and I met weekly to talk about issues, mutual concerns about our families, and pray for each other.

During this time, I realized how much God loved me. He sent this very special woman into my life as a means to develop a meaningful relationship with Him. Mentoring is all about developing meaningful relationships. Along with our study and prayertimes, we included fun outings, and time for just girl talk. Doris has influenced my life in a very positive way. She encouraged me to use my spiritual gifts of leadership and administration. With the pastor's approval, I formed several Bible studies for specialized groups of women within our church: singles, widows, divorced, college and career age, and seniors.

After 18 years of Doris mentoring me, we are closer than ever. She is the sister I never had and the best friend I always wanted. She has made a great difference in my life.

CLOSING
MATERIALS

THE JOURNEY ENDS

WE CONCLUDE OUR STUDY OF MARY AND MARTHA

LET'S PRAY A CLOSING PRAYER TOGETHER

Father, help us learn to balance the worship of Mary with the work of Martha. Let us not neglect the duties we have to those around us, but let us never neglect spending precious moments with You. Help us give freely to those who have less than us and always be open and alert to ways we can use our talents and gifts to further Your kingdom here on earth and populate the eternal kingdom. Help us to remember we are sisters in Christ with all Christian women. Help us learn to work unified, combining all the gifts, talents, and personalities You have given us. Thank You for the time we had together in this study. Helps us apply the lessons we learned to our lives and to working for Your kingdom. Amen.

JANET'S SUGGESTIONS

If this study touched a chord with you as it did with me, I highly recommend reading Joanna Weaver's book, *Having a Mary Heart in a Martha World*.

It's helpful in all your relationships to understand your personality type and spiritual giftedness. Service and ministry are much easier when you are functioning within your SHAPE. For more information on personalities, read Florence Littauer's book *Personality Plus*, and you can obtain personality tests at www.classervices.com or by calling 1-800-433-6633.

To learn more about SHAPE, read *The Purpose Driven® Church* by my pastor, Rick Warren.

For spiritual gift testing, I like Peter Wagner's *Finding Your Spiritual Gifts, A Wagner-Modified Houts Questionnaire* (Gospel Light).

To learn more about the miraculous rescue of missionaries Danya Curry and Heather Mercer that I recounted in Session Five, you can read their story in the book *Prisoners of Hope: The Story of Our Captivity and Freedom in Afghanistan* (authors, Dayna Curry, Heather Mercer, and Stacy Mattingly, WaterBrook Press).

You can read about the miraculous story of praying home my prodigal daughter, Kim, in *Praying for Your Prodigal Daughter: Hope, Help, & Encouragement for Hurting Parents* (Howard Books/Simon & Schuster). I also offer encouragement and tips to help parents of prodigals pray for their daughters.

My book *Dear God, They Say It's Cancer: A Companion Guide for Women on the Breast Cancer Journey* (Howard Books/Simon & Schuster), also cited earlier in this book, is my opportunity to mentor other breast-cancer sisters from my own journey.

Woman to Woman Mentoring: How to Start, Grow, And Maintain a Mentoring Ministry DVD Leader Kit is available at your local LifeWay bookstore or at www.lifeway.com or by calling: 1-800-458-2772.

Additional "Face-to-Face" Bible studies:
Face-to-Face with Naomi and Ruth: Together for the Journey
Face-to-Face with Elizabeth and Mary: Generation to Generation
Face-to-Face with Euodia and Syntyche: From Conflict to Community

To learn more about AHW Ministries, Janet's writing and speaking ministry, visit www.womantowomanmentoring.com.

LEADER'S GUIDE

FOR
GROUP-STUDY FACILITATORS
AND M&M'S

SUGGESTIONS FOR FACILITATORS

Congratulations! God has appointed you the awesome privilege of setting the pace and focus for this group. Regardless of how many groups you have facilitated, this group will be a new and unique experience. The Session Guide has suggestions and tips that have helped me, and I trust they also will benefit you. Change or adapt them as you wish, but they are a place to start.

ORGANIZING THE SESSIONS

Small groups generally meet in a home, and larger churchwide groups usually meet at the church or other facility. I suggest for the larger group that you form small groups by sitting everyone at round tables. Appoint or ask for a volunteer facilitator for each table and have the group sit together for the five sessions of this study. Then both small group leaders and large group table facilitators can use the following format:

1. Starting the Sessions—In my experience, members usually come in rushed, harried, and someone is always late—creating the perplexing dilemma of when to start? I suggest beginning on time because you are committed to ending on time. Don't wait for the last late person to arrive.

Waiting dishonors those who arrive on time and sets the precedent that it's OK to be a little late because they won't start without you anyway. Also, if you delay the start time, you may not finish the discussion.

2. Icebreakers — Each session has an "icebreaker" that is fun, interactive, helps the group become acquainted, and encourages on-time arrivals. It's an interactive activity they won't want to miss. The icebreaker also eases the group members out of their hectic day and into a study mode.

3. Format — Each session is comprised of: Opening Prayer, Icebreaker, Five Days of Selected Discussion Questions, Prayer, Fellowship.

4. The Session Guide provides you with:
♦ Preparation: what you need to do or get in advance.
♦ Icebreakers: to open each meeting.
♦ Underlined: the action you need to say or take.
♦ Ideas: to facilitate discussion and suggestions of answers that might be less obvious.
♦ Session name, day, and page number to identify area discussed.

5. Suggested time — Each session has nine numbered activities. Fifteen minutes on each number equals a two-hour meeting. This is a guideline to modify according to your time allotment. Let the Holy Spirit move and cover what seems applicable and pertinent to your group.

6. Facilitating discussion — Questions and Scriptures to discuss are only a suggestion to enhance what they already have studied on their own. Feel free to cover whatever material you or the group feel is pertinent. Think about ways to:
♦ Keep all engaged in conversation.
♦ Avoid "rabbit trails."
♦ Assure each one has a clear understanding of the points under discussion.
♦ Encourage members to stay accountable by doing their lesson and arriving on time.
Big job you say! You can do it with God's help and strength.

7. Prayertime — Prayer should be an ongoing and vital part of your group. Open and close your times together in prayer. There is a prayer at the end of each Session to pray together. Taking prayer requests can often get lengthy and be a source of gossip, if not handled properly. Let me share with you a way that works well in groups:
● At the end of your meeting, give each woman an index card and instruct her to write *one* prayer request, pertaining to the study, and hand the card to the leader/facilitator. Mix up the cards and have each person

pick one. If someone picks her own card, have her put it back in the pile and pick another one.

- When everyone has a card, go around the group (or table) and each person reads the name and prayer request on her card so others can write down the requests. They may want to use the Prayer & Praise Journal beginning on page 138.
- Instruct the group to hold hands, and in unison, pray the prayer request for the person whose card they have. This allows everyone to experience praying.
- Each woman takes home the card she received and prays for that person.
- As the leader/facilitator, pray between meetings for the group, your leadership, and ask God to mentor you and the members. And have fun!

8. Communion — You will offer communion during the last session (assuming doing so creates no problems in your church context). Remind the group that taking communion together as believers is significant and unifying in three ways:

- Proclaiming the Lord's death
- An opportunity for fellowship and unity
- An occasion for remembrance of Jesus

If there are nonbelievers, explain that communion is for believers. This is a perfect opportunity to ask if they would like to accept Jesus Christ as their Savior and pray the Salvation Prayer on page 28. If they are not ready, then ask them to sit quietly while the believers take communion. Ask someone to read aloud the Scriptures in Matthew 26:26–29 or Luke 22:14–20 and have the group partake of the juice and bread at the appropriate spot in the Scripture reading. Matthew 26:30 says, *"When they had sung a hymn they went out to the Mount of Olives."* Close the time of communion with a worship song.

9. Fellowship time — It's important for relationships to develop so group members feel comfortable sharing during discussions. A social time with refreshments provides a nice way to bring closure to the evening and allows time to chat. Encourage everyone to stay. Fellowship is part of the small group experience and allows larger groups to get to know other members.

M & M'S
Use the Session Guide for additional information and help in determining which questions to emphasize.

Face-to-Face with Mary and Martha

SESSION GUIDE
FACE-TO-FACE WITH MARY AND MARTHA:
SISTERS IN CHRIST

SESSION ONE—THEIR STORY
LEADER PREPARATION:

- Blank name tags and black felt pen.
- Birthday cake and candles.
- Personality tests for everyone. (Janet's Suggestions, page 122)
- Spiritual gifts tests for everyone. (Janet's Suggestions, page 122)

1. Opening Prayer: Hold hands as a group and **open** in prayer.

2. Icebreaker:

Q: **Hand out** blank name tags, cautioning group members **not** to put their own names on the name tags.

Q: **Instruct** them to write *Mary* or *Martha* on the name tags based on who they relate to most.

Q: Under "Mary" or "Martha," **have** them write *older, middle, younger,* or *only*, based on their relationship to their siblings. **Explain** that for this exercise, middle sisters are both older and younger, and "only" children are older.

Q: **Ask** them to wear these name tags during the group session.

Q: **Group together** the Marys and Marthas.

Q: **Give** both groups these questions to discuss and **have them** choose a spokesperson to report on their answers:

- How many are younger/older/middle/only sisters in each group?
- Why do you relate to the group of Marys or Marthas?

Q: **Gather** back as one group and **have** the spokesperson from each group report on the answers to the two questions.

Q: **Note and discuss** any patterns or correlations between the Marys and Marthas being younger or older sisters in their own family.

FIVE DAYS OF DISCUSSION QUESTIONS

3. Day One: How Does Mary and Martha's Story Relate to Us? Page 20

Q: **Ask** several people to read aloud Luke 10:38–42, John 11:1–48, and John 12:1–11.

Q: **Lead** a discussion of new things they learned about Mary, Martha, and Lazarus.

4. **Day Two: Chronological Age Versus Spiritual Age, Page 22**

Q: **Ask:** Are there any questions regarding What Is Mentoring? and Who Are M&M'S?

Q: **Read** in unison Titus 2:1–8 inserting the word *spiritually* before older and younger.

Q: **Emphasize** that mentoring is **not** limited by chronological age.

Q: Focusing on Titus 2:3–5, **ask** women to raise their hands if someone has taught them how to live a reverent life, not to gossip or be a slanderer, and that addictions are not good? Everyone should have her hand raised.

Q: While they still have their hands up **say,** "Congratulations you are all the older women. Now, what are you supposed to do with what you have been taught?"

Q: Their response should be: "Teach what we've been taught."

Q: **Point out** that mentoring is simply *teaching* what someone has *taught* you so you can *train* the next generation; so they can *teach* what they have been *taught* by you so they can *train* and on and on.

Q: **Ask:** How might chronological age difference influence the roles Mary and Martha took in Luke 10:38–42?

Q: **Point out** because Martha was older, she may have held onto more traditional values of the day that a woman's place was in the kitchen. Being younger, Mary may have been more of a risk-taker as she sat as a disciple at Jesus's feet—not a common role for women in that day.

Q: **Assure** they understand why chronological age does not make someone ready to mentor. Reasons: the person may not be a Christian or may be a new, immature, or backslidden Christian. Chronological age does not equate to spiritual age.

5. **Day Three: Celebrating Your Spiritual Birthday, Page 26**

Q: **Ask** each woman to share her chronological and born-again birthday. Not everyone will remember the exact day of becoming a Christian, but most will have a general idea.

Q: **Be sensitive** to any nonbelievers or seekers, who will only have a chronological birthday.

Q: **Ask** someone to read aloud John 11:25 and John 3:3–7. **Discuss** any "born again" questions.

Q: **Discuss** action verbs they located in Psalm 145:4–7 and the application to mentoring.

Q: **Ask** two or three volunteers to give their "elevator three-minute" born-again testimony.

Q: **Offer** the opportunity for any unbelievers to pray the Salvation Prayer. If someone does—make it a BIG celebration.

6. **Day Four: Sister to Sister, Page 30**

Q: **Have** several women with sisters describe a situation in their life similar to the one Mary and Martha experienced in Luke 10:38–42.

Instruct them to:

- **Focus** on their role in it. Were they happy the way they acted or reacted?
- How will they handle a similar situation differently next time?

Q: **Ask:** What did you learn from the verses about a quiet, gracious, and gentle spirit (page 31)? Is maintaining this attitude hard for any of you?

7. Day Five: Sisters in Christ, Page 33

Q: **Ask** the women to raise their hands if they have a mother… stepmother… or mother–in–law. How about a daughter-in-law? Aunt? Grandmother? Great Grandmother? Without taking a pause, **ask:** "How many of you have a mom?" A few questioning hands will go up as others stop and think about it.

Q: **Assure** them they all have a mom, even if she is no longer living.

Q: **Ask:** "If you all have a mom, what does that make you?" Response should be "daughters."

Q: **Say:** "We're all daughters with the same heavenly Father."

Q: **Ask:** "So what does that make all of us?" Answer: "Sisters."

Q: **Instruct:** Turn to the person next to you and say: "Hey, sis, we have the same Father!"

- Usual response is laughter, along with an "aha" from many of the women as they "get it."

Q: **Lead** a discussion on what it means to be "sisters in Christ."

8. PRAYERTIME (See Leader's Guide Page 125)

Q: Prayer requests, prayer partner exchange, and group prayer.

9. FELLOWSHIP AND REFRESHMENTS

Q: **Set out** a birthday cake with candles to celebrate their chronological and spiritual birthdays.

Q: **Give** everyone a personality and spiritual gifts test to complete and bring to the next meeting. **Ask** for a donation to cover the cost.

SESSION TWO–
WE ARE WONDERFULLY MADE–DIFFERENT
LEADER PREPARATION:

- Blank name tags and black felt pen.
- Personality and spiritual gifts tests for anyone who forgot to bring hers.

1. Opening Prayer: Hold hands as a group and open in prayer.

2. Icebreaker:

Q: **Hand out** blank name tags and **instruct** (like last week) to write *Mary* or *Martha*; *older/ middle/younger/only*, based on their relationship to their siblings.

Q: **Have them** add on the name tags their dominant personality type and spiritual gift.

Q: **Ask** them to wear these name tags during the group session.

Q: **Have** the four main personality types (pages 38–39) break into groups.

Q: **Instruct** each group to select a spokesperson to report back on:

● Common personality traits

● Number of Marys and Marthas in each group

● Number of younger/middle/older/only sisters in each group

● Spiritual gifts each group has in common

Q: **Regroup**, instructing the personality types to continue sitting together.

Q: **Ask** the spokespersons to report the answers to the four questions.

Q: **Lead** a short discussion of any correlations within each group in:

● personality type

● number of Marys and Marthas

● older/younger/middle/only sister position

● spiritual gifts

Q: **Stay** in the groups **and note** any similarities in how the four groups answer upcoming discussion questions.

3. Day One: Complementary Personalities, Page 38

Q: **Discuss** the group's assessments of Mary's and Martha's personality types. A consensus will probably place Mary as the Melancholy/Beaver and Martha as a Choleric/Lion. Others may disagree; so, explore their thinking.

Q: **Point out** that in addition to their roles in Luke 10:38–42, Martha aggressively ran out to meet Jesus, while Mary remained at home, quiet, contemplative, maybe depressed, See John 11:17–20.

Q: **Caution** that there is no "correct" personality. Knowing personalities helps us not take differences personally. We all can love and serve Jesus in a way that comes natural to us, and Jesus loves us all. He made us all different to complement each other.

Q: **Ask** three people to read Proverbs 14:12, 16:2, and 18:17. **Discuss** the verses together.

Q: **Ask:** How many are morning people and night people? Then **ask**, how many are married to the opposite or in a mentoring relationship with the opposite?

Q: **Point out** that associating with people who have personalities that are different from ours helps us learn to modify our own way of doing things to accommodate others and learn to work together.

Q: **Ask** for other examples from their own lives.

4. Day Two: Using Our Spiritual Gifts, Page 43

Q: **Assign** readers aloud of Romans 12:3–8; 1 Corinthians 7:7 and 12:1–12, 27–31; and 1 Peter 4:10–11.

Q: Referring to these Scriptures, **discuss** their answers for the questions on pages 43–44.

Q: **Assign** readers for Psalm 16:10 and Acts 2:22–28. **Discuss** the spiritual gifts they saw in Mary's anointing of Jesus.

Q: **Ask:** Do any of you struggle with being a Martha in the area of hospitality?

Q: **Assign** readers for Romans 12:9–13, 16:23, and 1 Peter 4:9 and **discuss** biblical hospitality.

Q: **Ask** if they do not have the gift of hospitality, how do they entertain?

5. **Day Three: Uniquely You for God's Glory, Page 47**

Q: **Discuss** how Mary was ministering within her SHAPE.

Q: **Ask:** What did you learn about the difference between discernment and judgment?

Q: **Discuss** how Martha might have been out of her SHAPE.

Q: **Ask:** Do you know your SHAPE, and are you using it for God's glory?

6. **Day Four: Making Better Choices, Page 51**

Q: **Have** the Marys go into the kitchen and the Marthas stay in the living room. (If not in a house go to two different areas of the room. **Instruct** each group to discuss the following questions:

● What was the better choice that Mary made?

● What are your excuses for not sitting more at the feet of Jesus?

● How do we compromise service for the Lord when we don't spend time with Him first?

● What can you do to choose the "better way" or "better part"?

7. **Day Five: Learning from Our Mistakes, Page 55**

Q: **Reconvene** and stay in new groups to **discuss** how Martha changed between the two meals she prepared (Luke 10:38–42 and John 12:1–8). Be sure they note that after listening to the words of Jesus, Martha displays spiritual growth and maturity.

Q: **Ask:** Has spiritual maturity changed your practice of hospitality? If so, how?

Q: **Ask** someone to read Proverbs 17:1. **Discuss** how this verse spoke to each of them.

Q: **Assign** readers for Acts 16:13–15 and Hebrews 13:1–2.

Q: **Invite** several women to share blessings they've received from opening up their homes for ministry; **ask** others to share what they might have missed by thinking they or their houses were not ready for God's use.

8. **PRAYERTIME**

Q: Prayer requests, prayer partner exchange, and group prayer.

closing materials

9. FELLOWSHIP AND REFRESHMENTS

Q: **Tell** them to save their name tags and bring them to next session.

SESSION THREE–FIRST THINGS FIRST
LEADER PREPARATION:

● Blank name tags and black felt pen for those who forgot their name tags: they should fill them out again as in Session Two.

1. Opening Prayer: Hold hands as a group and **open** in prayer.

2. Icebreaker:

Q: **Have** them put on their name tags from last session.

Q: **Describe** a scenario where they have just learned Jesus is in town and they invited Him and His disciples to come to dinner tonight.

Q: **Break** into two groups of Marys and Marthas.

Q: **Ask** each group to make a list of what they would do to prepare, and in what order?

Q: **Reconvene** and spokespersons from each group read their lists and see how the in-order to-do lists coordinate with characteristics of the personality types and spiritual giftedness in the two groups.

3. Day One: Setting Priorities, Page 60

Q: **Ask:** How did Mary and Martha each apply the Great Commandment (Matthew 22:37–40)?

Q: **Read** John 1:1. **Ask** how this verse relates to the importance of a quiet time?

Q: **Ask** each group member how she answered: *How can you put Jesus first in your life, your work, and the work you do for Him?*

4. Day Two: Assigning Kingdom Value, Page 64

Q: **Read** Matthew 4:4 and Luke 12:29–34.

Q: **Lead** a discussion of what kingdom value means to them and how they could use it to prioritize their life.

5. Day Three: Balancing Work and Worship, Page 67

Q: **Ask** several volunteers to share a time they focused on *working for* the Lord and missed out on *worshipping* the Lord. **Encourage** them to explain what they learned from this experience.

Q: **Ask:** How Matthew 11:28–30 can help you achieve balance?

Q: **Point out** that Carley in the Personal Parable understood balancing work and worship.

6. **Day Four: Busting Busyness, Page 70**
Q: **Ask:** How are your doing with a daily quiet time?
Q: **Ask** those who are doing well to share tips that helped them be consistent in quiet times.
Q: **Personalize** aloud together Psalm 63:1–8.
Q: **Ask:** Why do we feel a need to be busy?
Q: **Ask:** How will you go about busting busyness?

7. **Day Five: Serving Joyfully and Selflessly, Page 74**
Q: **Lead** a discussion of the verses on pride and humility.
Q: **Discuss** how Mary role modeled gracious humility to Martha's pride and anger.
Q: **Ask:** How can you tell if you're busy working *for* the Lord or serving *with* the Lord?
Q: **Ask** several to share "warning lights" that signal them they have lost perspective.

8. **PRAYERTIME**
Q: Prayer requests, prayer partner exchange, and group prayer.

9. **FELLOWSHIP AND REFRESHMENTS**

SESSION FOUR–IT'S A MIRACLE!
LEADER PREPARATION:

● **Prepare** a beverage and **have** cups or glasses and napkins ready, but not out.
● **Tell** everyone as they come in that you won't be having liquid beverage until group starts.

1. **Opening Prayer: Hold hands** as a group and **open** in prayer.

2. **Icebreaker:**
Q: **Set out** the beverages, cups or glasses, and napkins.
Q: **Have** the Marys serve beverages to the Marthas.
Q: **Ask** the Marthas to reveal how it felt to be sitting and being served. Could they do it, or did they want to get up and help or make sure the Marys were serving correctly?
Q: **Ask** the Marys how it felt to be in a servant's role.

3. **Day One: A Test of Faith, Page 80**
Q: **Ask:** Why wasn't Martha's faith complete in John 11:21–24? Some answers: she didn't believe Jesus could heal without being physically there, she didn't believe Jesus could resurrect Lazarus before the great resurrection (which is understandable), she doubted Jesus's plan.

closing materials

Q: **Facilitate** a discussion of doubt versus faith reviewing the Scriptures on page 81.

Q: **Practice together** prayerfully putting on the armor of God, as described in Ephesians 6:10–18.

Q: **Ask:** How do you think Martha's encounters with Jesus in John 11:1–45 matured her faith?

Q: **Invite** several to share how an encounter with Jesus grew their faith.

4. Day Two: Waiting Together, Page 84

Q: **Lead** a discussion of what they think each sister was thinking when Jesus didn't arrive at the time they expected Him.

Q: Then **ask:** What would be going through your minds in a similar situation?

Q: **Read** aloud John 11:20 and **discuss** their answers to how each sister reacted to the delay and how it correlates with her personality.

Q: **Ask** for volunteers who would like to share a time of waiting on the Lord.

Q: **Look** at John 11:33–35, 38 and **discuss** how making us wait is painful for Jesus too.

Q: **Pray** together aloud Psalm 33:20–22 and Psalm 130:5,7.

5. Day Three: Crisis Mentoring, Page 87

Q: **Discuss** how Mary's moment of doubt and Paul's struggle with sin gives them confidence that you don't have to be perfect to mentor or be a role model.

Q: **Look** at the Personal Parable on page 88 and **discuss** what Pastor Greg Laurie knows and that Mary and Martha were soon to find out.

6. Day Four: God Always Has a Plan, Page 90

Q: **Ask** for several examples of seeing God's plan at work in situations that looked impossible.

Q: **Pray** over anyone who currently needs a "resurrection."

Q: **Pray** together Job 42:2.

Q: **Read** Proverbs 19:21 and Jeremiah 29:11 and **ask** if they believe God's promise.

Q: **Discuss** how Proverbs 16:3 can help us align our plans with God's plans.

7. Day Five: God Still Works Miracles! Page 93

Q: **Ask** someone to give her definition of a *miracle*, then **have** someone look up the dictionary's definition.

Q: **Stress** a miracle is something we see or experience in the physical world, which surpasses all known human or natural powers—it's supernatural. A "wonderful thing; a marvel," says one dictionary.

Q: **Ask:** Why do people more readily see God in something when it looks impossible?

Q: **Break** the group into small groups of 2, 3, or 4 depending on the size of the group. **Give** each group one of the following questions and **have** them pick a spokesperson to report to the group.

- What was the purpose of the miracle feeding of the more than 5,000?
- What was the purpose of the healing of the blind man?
- What was the purpose of Jesus allowing Lazarus and Dorcas to die?
- What is the common purpose—past and present—of all miracles?

Q: **Reconvene** and **ask** the spokespersons to give a brief summary of their group's answers. They should conclude that the purpose in all miracles is to point people to Jesus.

Q: **Point out** that the effect a miracle has on someone depends on her spiritual condition.

Q: **Facilitate** discussion of the quote from the *Believer's Bible Commentary*.

8. PRAYERTIME

Q: Prayer requests, prayer partner exchange, and group prayer.

9. FELLOWSHIP AND REFRESHMENTS

SESSION FIVE–SACRIFICE UNTO THE LORD
LEADER PREPARATION:

- **Bring** an array of fragrances i.e.; sweet smelling perfume, flowers that have a strong smell, an open jar of sauerkraut, fresh baked cookies right out of the oven, something that has spoiled or gone rancid, a bag of garbage from the kitchen…do you get the idea?
- **Have ready** a fresh baked loaf of bread from either a breadmaker or right out of the oven. Do not use bread at this time.
- **Fill** small cups with grape juice for communion and **use** the fresh baked bread.
- **Have** a song ready to sing after communion.

1. Opening Prayer: **Hold** hands as a group and **open** in prayer.

2. Icebreaker:

Q: **Break** the group into as many groups as you have fragrances.

Q: **Give** each group one of the aroma filled items.

Q: **Ask** them to pick a spokesperson to report the consensus on answers to these questions:

- What is your reaction to this smell?
- Is it a smell that imparts value or disgust?
- If it is a disgusting smell, was it always bad or did something happen to turn a good smell to bad?
- Would you want this smell in your home?

closing materials

- Are all "bad" smells bad and "good" smells good for you? (For example, someone could be allergic to the smell of flowers or perfume).
- Do you want your life to have an aroma like the item you have in your group? Why or why not?
- How can this experience remind you of the fragrance your life is to be to God?

Q: **Reconvene** and **ask** each spokesperson to give a report.

3. Day One: Miracles May Require Sacrifice, Page 100

Q: **Compare** the correlation between Jesus waiting to perform a miracle with Lazarus and the miracle of the freeing of the eight Christian aides from a prison in Afghanistan. Use the questions in the study (page 102) as a guide to this discussion. Conclude that Jesus often waits to intervene to draw attention to the impossible circumstance, so that when He does perform a miracle, many witnesses will believe in Him and believers will tell others of the wonders they have seen.

Q: **Ask** volunteers to share the "answered prayer" testimony they wrote.

4. Day Two: The Ultimate Sacrifice, Page 105

Q: **Discuss** Hebrews 9:24–28, Romans 12:1 and Ephesians 5:1.

Q: **Ask** for volunteers to share the areas of sacrifice to the Lord they struggle with.

Q: **Read** aloud John 15:12–13, 17, and **lead** a discussion of how Jesus's sacrifice for us should influence our sacrificing for the Lord and others.

Q: If there is a mentor or former mentor in the group **ask** her to describe the blessings she received from the sacrifice of her time and energy in mentoring.

Q: **Instruct** them to write down a sacrifice they are willing to make for the Lord this week.

Q: **Give** them a few moments, then **ask** if any would like to share.

5. Day Three: The Fragrance of Sacrifice, Page 109

Q: **Discuss** the Old Testament and New Testament verses on pages 109–110.

Q: **Pose** this question to the group: "How is your life a sweet fragrance or aroma to the Lord?"

Q: **Bring** out a washbasin filled with perfumed water.

Q: **Invite** one of the women to put her feet in the basin and **ask** if one of the other ladies would like to wash her feet. If no one responds, you do it.

Q: **Proceed** with either you washing everyone's feet or them washing each other's feet.

Q: **Maintain** a sacred sacrificial atmosphere, even if they are nervous.

Q: When they finish, **spray** perfume into the room, and **bring** in a loaf of fresh baked bread (bread from a bread machine or oven would be perfect—this bread is for communion later).

Q: **Have** them close their eyes and smell the two fragrances described in John 12:1–8.

Q: **Ask:** How do the two aromas compliment each other?

Q: **Ask** the women to describe what it felt like having someone wash your feet and sacrificially washing someone else's feet.

6. **Day Four: Risky Sacrifice, Page 112**

Q: **Remind** the group that no matter what others say about our service or our worship of Jesus, what counts is what pleases the Lord. It is God's approval that matters.

Q: **Discuss** what Mary, Martha, and Lazarus each risked by knowing Jesus.

Q: **Ask** if anyone wants to share a risk she took for Jesus.

7. **Day Five: Teamwork Is Sacrifice, Page 115**

Q: **Lead** a discussion of ways they saw the sisters working together during Lazarus's illness. Some answers are: together they sent word to Jesus that their brother was ill, they agreed to turn to Jesus for help, they both expected Jesus to be prompt, they both were convinced that Jesus could heal Lazarus, Martha served while Mary anointed.

Q: **Break** into pairs. **Ask** the pairs to first tell each other something they value in her being a part of the group and then to pray for each other.

Q: **Reconvene** and **lead** a discussion of ways they have seen the group work as a team during this study.

Q: **Look** together over Janet's Suggestions on page 122–123 and **encourage** each of them to select something to do for further study.

8. **PRAYERTIME**

Q: **Review** the answers to prayer they have seen during this study.

Q: Then **take** communion together (see page 126) using the fresh baked bread and juice.

Q: **Sing** a worship song together.

Q: **Pray** in unison the closing prayer on page 122.

9. **FELLOWSHIP AND REFRESHMENTS**

Q: **Talk** about the study the group wants to do next. **See** page 123 for additional "Face-to-Face" Bible study series.

PRAYER & PRAISE JOURNAL

PRAYER & PRAISE JOURNAL

PRAYER & PRAISE JOURNAL

PRAYER & PRAISE JOURNAL

PRAYER & PRAISE JOURNAL